gourd girls

Priscilla Wilson

MT YONAH PRESS

For information: Mt. Yonah Press, 2319 Duncan Bridge Road, Sautee, GA 30571

ISBN: 096511967X
Library of Congress Control Number: 2005931009

Designed by Linda Crittenden

Foreword

When Janice Lymburner and I first began using the expression "the gourd life," it was just one of many puns that are both a delight and an occupational hazard of our business. We saw it as a kind of fool's version of the proverbial "good life."

But sometime in the last 20-odd years, we began to view the gourd life as more than a joke. It became a metaphor for the kind of life to which we aspire: one in which everyone gets to be fully herself or himself and to do something fulfilling, even if it isn't on society's approved list. It is an ideal reality in which work, play, friendships, family life, and spirituality are all woven into one fabric - a fabric in which colors may blend and harmonize in an infinite number of ways.

The story that follows is woven of many threads. When I began writing it down, I saw that I had neither the desire nor the ability to pull the strands apart. Although our literal gourd life—the story of Gourdcraft Originals, Inc.—is the main thread of my narrative, it is not the only one. For this I make no apologies but defer to William Butler Yeats:

> O chestnut tree, great rooted blossomer,
> Are you the leaf, the blossom or the bole?
> O body swayed to music, O brightening glance,
> How can we know the dancer from the dance?

>   from "Among School Children"

gourd [gôrd] n. **1.** Any of several trailing or climbing plants related to the pumpkin, squash, and cucumber and bearing fruits with a hard rind. **2.** The fruit of such a plant, often of irregular and unusual shape. **3.** The dried and hollowed-out shells of these fruits, often used as containers, drinking utensils, floats, toys, musical instruments, or to serve many other purposes.

Idiom: out of (one's) gourd *Slang* Very foolish; crazy.

gourd girls

Emory Jones

Breaking Ground

I began my career as a gourd farmer on a sparkling April morning in 1977. Shivering a little with cold and excitement, I drove my tan-and-white Volkswagen van four miles south from Cleveland on old Georgia Highway 75 and turned onto the narrow dirt road that led into the Smith property. The drive ended in front of a small white frame farmhouse with an impressive patch of bamboo growing to the right of it. I parked on the grass beside the bamboo and got out, squinting across the drive toward a rectangular patch of ground that looked like an overgrown football field bordered by tall Virginia pines on three sides.

A beat-up tan Toyota truck pulled up beside me, and a dark-haired, bearded guy in a straw fedora, jeans, and a shapeless gray T-shirt got out. It was hard to tell about his age, but I thought he looked a little younger than my 26 years. Steve Smith and I introduced ourselves and stood in the warmth of the morning sun making small talk.

He had phoned me two nights before in response to a notice I'd placed on the bulletin board at the White County Farmers' Exchange: "*Want to rent: ten acres of farmland.*" Fortunately for me, no one with 10 acres had responded, but Steve had wondered if I'd be interested in a 2-acre plot on his family's farm in Mossy Creek. He hadn't laughed at me or even seemed surprised when I'd told him we planned to grow gourds on the land. The rent, he'd told me, would be $10 an acre for a year.

Steve was in no particular hurry to get down to business that morning. He wanted to show me the two pigs he was raising in a recently built pen to the left of the field.

"What are their names?" I asked, trying to seem interested in spite of my impatience to talk about gourd farming.

"Pork Chop and Chitlin," said Steve, laughing a little. I tried to hide my discomfort at seeing—up close for the first time in my life—animals doomed to be eaten.

I had grown up in the medium-sized south Georgia town of Valdosta and had been sheltered from realities that country people take for granted. Even in the three years I had lived in Cleveland, population 1,500, I had been teaching school and had not learned much about rural life.

We walked a little way into the field, which to my untrained eyes looked fine for growing gourds. Steve pointed out the swamp grass, red-nosed briars, and other heavy-duty weeds with which we would have to contend, but I was unconcerned. There was no way he could have understood how little I knew about farming.

"I'll take it!" I told him. "What do we do now?"

Steve gave me a funny look. He was beginning to grasp the depth of my ignorance. He began explaining to me about the need to break up the ground before planting and soon found himself agreeing to harrow the field. Before the morning was over, he let me drive the 1949 gray-and- red Ford 8-N tractor myself. Oblivious to the huge clods of swamp grass that resisted the harrows, I was in heaven as I sat on that hard metal seat and experienced for the first time the rich, earthy smell that always rises when ground is broken. The smell, the noise of the old tractor engine, the vibrations that carried all the way through my body, and the warmth of the sun were all that existed for me.

When I left my high school teaching job and started making crafts from gourds the summer of 1976, it had been too late in the season to plant a crop, but Janice Lymburner and I had quickly come to the conclusion that we would plant our own field of gourds the following spring. The idea made sense from the standpoint of supplying me with raw material for use in my fledgling business, and we were both just plain in love with the idea of being farmers.

Janice, who was teaching first grade at the time, had been co-dreamer and unofficial partner in my little enterprise from the start. A nursery-man's daughter who'd grown up alongside the roses, azaleas, and camel-lias at Lymburner's Nursery out on Buford Highway in Atlanta, she had both horticultural and entrepreneurial genes. She saw gourd farming as an important part of the ground-breaking business that we envisioned— a business that would combine art and agriculture.

It was Janice's idea to invite a few friends to help us plant the gourds. We scheduled planting day for the Saturday after Steve and I harrowed the field, and he agreed to come and show us how to do the job.

On the day before, I went to the field by myself with sticks and string and divided the field into 17 small plots. Each plot would be planted in seed of a different kind of gourd: dipper, birdhouse, bushel, snake, and luffa gourds, among others. I understood that most of the kinds of gourds we were planting, even though they had different shapes, were the same species and therefore could be cross-pollinated by insects, but I planned to prevent that problem while increasing production by hand-pollinating the blooms. I had read about how to tell the male blooms from the female ones and how to dust the female blooms with pollen using an artist's paint brush.

The next day Janice and I showed up at the field with our close friend and roommate, Mildred Neville, and three other adventurous friends. We brought hoes, bags of gourd seed I'd been saving, brand-new sun hats from Cleveland's only Jiffy store, and plenty of energy—but none of us had the faintest idea how to plant a crop. I had read everything I could find about how to grow gourds. But as I stood there with that foreign object called a hoe in one hand and several bread bags of carefully saved seed in the other, I understood the profound inadequacy of book learning.

"How do we do it?" Six city-slicker women gathered around Steve, waiting expectantly for instructions.

He showed us how to prepare each hill with a hoe by chopping and mixing until the soil was loose and fine. We hacked at the huge clods of swamp grass with boundless energy and somehow managed to plant the better part of two acres that day. To the best of my recollection, we placed each seed in the ground individually, eye down, as my reading material had recommended. We then hand-patted the dirt and laughingly spoke words of encouragement over each hill.

"I know how to wield a hoe now," I wrote in my journal a few days

First planting

later. I thought I was a real farmer.

Steve had told us the gourds would take a long time to germinate, so Janice and I forced ourselves to wait two interminable weeks before we went back to the field to look for signs of life. We were rewarded by the sight of several lovely sprouts stretching in the sun and many more pushing their way through the soil. We walked up and down the rows, excitedly checking every single hill for signs of the ground cracking. In those moments we experienced the same joy that has always kept farmers going, the joy of taking part in a miracle. Of course we saw only the miraculous gourd sprouts and failed to notice the army of weeds surrounding them and outnumbering them at least a million to one.

❧

Janice, Mildred, and I were living at that time in the basement apartment of a rambling green frame house in Cleveland owned by Mildred's parents. Our living space left something to be desired, but the monthly rent of $12.50 each was a bargain even in 1977—and we had a priceless view from our living room window of the rock face of nearby Mount Yonah. Standing alone near the center of White County, Yonah is a distinctive mountain that newcomers quickly come to know and love. In the three years I'd been living in that space, I had often turned a searching gaze there.

But now I was happily focused on lower ground. Every morning after Janice and Mildred left for their "real jobs," I drove the VW bus the four miles from Cleveland to the farm, listening to "Testimony Time" on Cleveland's only radio station. I took sharp enthusiasm, a dull hoe, and a sack lunch to my job site and spent long, beautiful days hoeing.

It didn't take long to grasp the truth about the weeds: some of them were already several inches tall and depriving our precious sprouts of sunlight. Unless we could get them under control pretty quickly, our gourds wouldn't stand a chance. Janice helped me hoe on afternoons and Saturdays, but as the weeks went by we were losing ground fast.

After school was out for Janice we escalated our attack. Our weapons included a borrowed rototiller, which went only 10 yards before its tines became so entangled in briars that the machine couldn't move; a great big rented weed-eater, which pruned the ragweeds much to their liking but left us feeling as though we had been beat up by thugs; and, eventually, a hundred feet of black plastic mulch that we tried to prop on weeds already two feet high. They loved the shade.

When a small percentage of our struggling vines finally began to bloom amid the jungle of briars and ragweeds, I tried to pollinate them with artist's paintbrushes as planned—and quickly saw that hand-pollination wasn't such a good idea after all. I couldn't even get close to most of the blooms through the tangle of weeds. I had no choice but to take what nature decided to give me by way of pollination.

Sometime about midsummer Janice convinced me that we had done all we could. The pitiful gourd vines that were still surviving by that time were climbing on the weeds, so we could no longer attack the weeds without harming the gourds. With great relief we gave up the fight and resolved to do better the next year.

The following winter we harvested our first crop of about 200 tiny gourds. Twenty-eight years later we still have a few of them; they're not good for much except laughs. After that first season we had nowhere to go but up.

John Kollock

Trash and Treasure

*T*he unlikely chain of events leading up to that early farming fiasco actually began three years earlier during my first year of teaching school in nearby Dahlonega. I was miserable as a high school teacher almost from the start, and I had begun to fantasize about starting some kind of fun business that would allow me to breathe and be self-sufficient. I was always talking about some impractical idea or another designed to get me out of the classroom, and my quest for the right business idea became a standing joke with friends and family.

At one point, in response to a newspaper ad seeking people interested in worm farming, I went to an office in downtown Atlanta and met with a worm salesman. Looking surprisingly clean and professional in coat and tie, the man showed me a sample tabletop worm-farm-in-a-box and outlined what my investment in breeder worms would need to be. Then, half-heartedly it seemed to me, he tried to explain how I could make big dollars raising bait. I couldn't get back to the mountains fast enough with a new story to tell.

Another idea I talked about a good deal was a picnic-basket-catering business—but I barely knew how to cook. Then, too, I fantasized, as most English majors do, about writing the *great American novel*. But, sorely lacking in life experience, I couldn't begin to think of a plot.

Then one summer day after my first year of teaching, Janice and I were riding around in the country near Highlands, North Carolina, when she mentioned that she wanted to stop at a roadside stand and look for a gourd to make a planter for her mother. The gourd planter idea had come to her out of the blue, though Janice wasn't ordinarily a crafty person. We found a ramshackle vegetable stand on Highway 64 somewhere among the hairpin curves between Highlands and Cashiers. An old guy sat there wearing the requisite pair of overalls unbuttoned on the sides, deadpan expression, and tobacco stain down one side of his mouth. "What can I help you 'uns with?"

When Janice asked if he had any gourds, he led us around behind his shack and pointed to a pile of large, moldy, pear-shaped objects, most of them about 8–10 inches in diameter. They looked like garbage. Amazingly, Janice—who is something of a clean freak—picked up a filthy gourd out of the pile and talked me into choosing one, too. Though they looked moldy on the outside, I could tell by the feel and weight of the one I picked up that it was dry, hollow, and sturdy. The man told us how to clean the gourds by soaking them in water and then scraping and scrubbing off the moldy outer skin. He assured us that soaking would soften only the skins, not the gourds themselves.

I know now that we were lucky to have such good instruction. Many people mistakenly think gourds have to be cleaned dry with steel wool or sandpaper. That method is a prescription for insanity, requiring many hours to clean one gourd.

The next afternoon we filled up an old washtub outside and floated the gourds in it for a while to soak them on one side. Then we scraped the wet parts with kitchen knives while holding the dry sides down in the water. The skin came off in strips like the skin of a potato comes off when scraped—except that the surface underneath the gourd skin was un-yielding. The experience was something like stripping an antique piece of furniture; it felt very satisfying to see the slick, gleaming, honey-colored shells appear as the outer skin came off. After we had scraped off most of the skin, we scrubbed the gourds all over with pot scrubbers.

"I'm going to ask Mildred's father to cut mine," Janice announced as she finished cleaning her gourd.

"Not me," I responded with uncharacteristic decisiveness. "I'm going to cut my own!"

After a brief failed attempt at cutting the gourd with a pocketknife, I

Scraping the skin off of a gourd

realized a saw was needed for the job; the shell was like wood. I found a small handsaw in Mr. Neville's workshop and inserted its blade into the crude slot I had made with the knife. I cut a simple round hole about six inches in diameter in the front of the gourd, large enough to insert a potted plant. As I sawed that first gourd, the proverbial wheels began turning in my head. I saw pictures, albeit fuzzy ones, of myself as a gourd crafter.

Craft shows were rising in popularity in the 1970s, and I realized that no one was using gourds as a craft material. I was captivated by the idea of inventing a new medium. Had I known the truth about the 3,000-year history of gourd art, I probably would not have been interested. But I was blissfully ignorant of any gourdcrafts more sophisticated than the dippers and birdhouses that are traditional in the southeastern United States.

I ended up cutting Janice's gourd as well as mine. The gourd walls were about a quarter of an inch thick. We pulled out the clumps of dry, spongy pulp along with hundreds of seeds, leaving the gourds entirely hollow inside. Then we used Mr. Neville's hand drill to make holes in the tops of the gourds through which we threaded some twine so that the planters could hang. Both of us eventually gave the planters to our mothers, who seemed to think they were charming.

Soon I was telling my friends and family that I was going to start a gourd business, and they thought this the funniest idea yet. Nevertheless, I was giving the idea serious thought as I began my second year of teaching. The following spring I turned down the new contract that was offered me, and people began giving me worried looks. The idea of a gourd business was no longer all that funny.

My parents must have been especially worried about me in view of the fact that my now-aborted teaching career had been the second false start for me in three years out of college, but they'd always tried to convey their acceptance of whatever I wanted to do. Janice and Mildred, both of whom were several years older than me and wise beyond their years, did not try to encourage or discourage me from pursuing the gourd business idea in those earliest days. If they were worried about me, they didn't show it.

So in the bicentennial year of 1976 I declared my own independence. My first act as a would-be gourd entrepreneur during that summer was to run an ad in *The Farmers and Consumers Market Bulletin* published by the Georgia Department of Agriculture: "Wanted to buy—cured gourds." Soon I received a letter from Flora Richards of Morganton, Georgia. I still have Mrs. Richards' letter:

> *Dear Sir I have severl gords around one hunderd an fifty of them all sizes at fifty cents a pice I Live a bout fore miles from Morganton on 76 hiway some gords are hangin one the side of the Road*
>
> *Mrs. Fred E. Richards*
> *no sunday sails*

The town of Morganton, near the Georgia-Tennessee line, is only a little more than an hour's drive north and west of Cleveland. I headed there at my first opportunity, never doubting that I would find the place or find its owners at home. The small, well-kept white farmhouse sat up on a hill to the left of Highway 76; the much larger unpainted barn was a stone's throw off to the right of the house. Flora Richards came out to greet me. A small woman with her white hair in a bun, she looked exactly the part of a character in *Foxfire*—which I was reading at the time like the good student of mountain life I wanted to be—right down to the apron she was wearing over her cotton shirtwaist dress. She was friendly in a business-like way as she directed me to the barn and told me to let her know if I decided to buy some gourds.

I was enchanted as I entered the old, dark, sweet-smelling temple where gourds of many shapes lay in a pile of hay like ancient treasures waiting to be discovered, spotlighted in shafts of sun coming through cracks in the barn wall. I bought all 150 of them and hung around trying to strike up a friendship with Mrs. Richards. She began to warm up to me

A barn full of treasures

and gave me a tiny potted plant she called Jacob's tears. I went back to visit Mr. and Mrs. Richards twice more that summer, once taking them a bushel of peaches. They were the first of many farming people who were to inspire me through the years and show me who I wanted to be. Janice and I still cherish one of the Richards gourds that hangs beside our fireplace.

I eagerly began cleaning my new treasures, revealing beautiful golden shells as the skins slipped away. But once I had cleaned them, I didn't know what to make with the gourds. I've always been good at vague fantasies, but moving into the realm of reality can be hard for me. For lack of knowing what else

to do, I made simple hanging planters, but I felt unsatisfied and doubted whether I had the imagination for the business I was trying to start.

As the new school year approached and Janice excitedly made plans for her first year of teaching first grade, I began wondering in earnest whether I was serious about the gourd business or whether it was indeed a joke that had gone too far. At the root of my discomfort, along with doubts about my abilities, was the realization that if I became a craftsperson I would no longer be in a helping profession as I had always expected to be.

One day I was talking with Mildred, who happened to be a psychologist as well as a caring friend, about my dilemma. She said something very helpful that is good advice for anyone engaged in a struggle with crazy dreams and strange leadings: "Why don't you just think of it as something you're doing for *now*?" she asked. "Then, later, if you don't want to do it anymore, you won't have to. You might even have a saleable business by then." Her words made sense and made my decision easier to live with, though I was never to shake my doubts entirely.

I couldn't comprehend how young I was or how easily and often I could have changed paths in the years to come. Now, 29 years later, I still fantasize from time to time about how I might have helped humankind in some large and important way. But for the most part I've learned that the needs of human beings are so vast and so diverse that each of us can serve in an infinite number of ways and in as unlikely a niche as we can create for ourselves. In August 1976, I wrote in my journal:

> I wonder if I should keep listening to the free spirit side of
> me. . . . Maybe I'm about to create something, and this is
> the painful labor stage. . . . Maybe I'll never do anything
> special if I don't listen to the reckless part.

Day by day the reckless part won out. Each morning when Janice went to school and Mildred to her job with the Georgia Department of Corrections, I cleaned a batch of gourds and then stared at them, wondering what to do next. Gradually I began making a variety of items: fireplace match holders, bookends, weed vases, and desk caddies. I weighted some gourds with plaster of Paris for bookends and inserted corks in the bottoms of others to make them sit at desired angles so that they could serve as pencil holders or table planters.

I had no thought of embellishing the gourds; they were beautiful in their natural state. But I liked the idea of making items that could be useful in people's daily lives. After deciding on *Gourdcraft Originals* as a name for the business, I wrote the following statement, which was printed on my first card:

> In our highly industrialized society, we need reminders
> of nature's ingenuity and special kind of beauty that
> factories simply can't re-create. Gourdcraft Originals
> make beautiful reminders.

Magic Trunk

With Janice's support and promise to accompany me, I signed up for my first craft show, the Indian Summer Festival, in late September 1976. My choice was based on the low booth fee of $10 and the fact that the show would be in Murphy, North Carolina, only about 50 miles north of us. As it turned out, price and proximity were the only things the show had going for it. Held in an open-air farmers' market on Highway 64, it boasted maybe 25 exhibitors, most of whom were selling what we now describe as loving-hands work: crocheted toilet paper holders, styrofoam puppets, primitive wood potato bins, and routed "Welcome Friends" signs. I suppose we fit right in with my primitive Gourdcraft Originals displayed on a Sears metal folding table draped in calico fabric. Attendance at the show was sparse, but fortunately a few people saw through my amateurish display to the potential it represented. Their encouragement and $50 in sales went a long way with me.

The following month we exhibited in the Cleveland Fall Festival, which provided a similar venue right at home. It also introduced us to Mr. L. S. "Lars" Larsen, who will always be high on our list of gourd characters.

Mr. Larsen must have been surprised and disturbed when he came upon our display at the festival. Having retired to White County many years before, he had become known for growing gourds and especially for tying the very long-handled ones in knots as they grew. He had never expected to share his county-gourd-man distinction with two young women. So he burst my bubble: "You know you're not the first people to do this kind of thing, don't you? They've been doing this in Peru for 3,000 years," he informed us with a bitter laugh. Sensitivity and tact were never Mr. Larsen's best virtues.

"And I'll bet you don't even know there's an American Gourd Society," he continued. "They've been around since the 1930s. You're nothing new."

Miraculously, I did not lose my enthusiasm for gourds as a result of hearing this information. My fascination with the medium had taken root free of outside influences, and even at this early stage in my artistic journey, I understood the importance of naïveté in my initial motivation and future creative life. Moreover, Mr. Larsen got over his jealousy and became our friend. Two of his knotted gourds hold places of honor in our museum today and have fascinated thousands of visitors over the years.

Emory Jones

One of Mr. Larsen's knotted gourds

Mr. Larsen paid Janice and me many visits during the next eight years that he remained healthy. When least expected, he'd pull into our driveway in his faded gold Dodge Colt, slowly maneuver his stooped body out of the car, and open his trunk, which we began to see as a magic trunk of sorts. I don't think he ever said "Hello" or answered our inquiries about his well-being. He simply began pulling wondrous things from the trunk.

Gourds were among the staples of his museum-on-wheels, but there were many other interesting plant materials as well. "Did you ever see one of these?" he'd ask by way of greeting, holding up a strange-looking seed pod. "This is from the unicorn plant." The unicorn was one of his favorites, as was the udder plant. The latter had a yellow fruit that looked like a cow's

Mr. Larsen with a watermelon harvest

udder and intrigued Mr. Larsen. I've never seen one since. Before we could ask questions about these fascinating fruits, he was on to more items for show and tell. He usually kept several knotted gourd specimens as part of his traveling show as well as other gourds that held special interest for him: luffas, crown-of-thorns, eggs, and other oddities.

In addition to the gourds, Mr. Larsen's trunk often held a miniature chair or two he'd made from Coke cans; several funky animals he'd made from hickory nuts, teasel pods, or pine knots; and a supply of dried money plant, which he freely shared. Just when I thought I'd seen all his tricks, he'd surprise us. After he was past 90 he showed us a quilt he was making.

Mr. Larsen was painting wooden watermelon wedges long before folk art became fashionable. Once he staged a photograph of himself dressed as a woodsman "harvesting" watermelons. He had painted not only wooden wedges to look like pieces of watermelon but also the tree trunk from which they had been cut. The snapshot should have won some kind of award, but instead it held a place of honor in his magic trunk.

The trunk was Mr. Larsen's trademark and calling card, but the fascination it represented spilled into every part of his life. The man had a passion for growing fruits, vegetables, and flowers of every kind; for playing the concertina; for photographing wildflowers; for engineering his diet to get the most benefit for an aging body; and for birds of all kinds. How many other passions could he have named about which I was unaware? I now see that what made the trunk so magical was its power to rekindle that passion for life years later in the hearts of those who remember it.

After the Cleveland Fall Festival where we met Mr. Larsen, we next exhibited the contents of our own expanding magic trunk in the antique and craft fairs held monthly at Lakewood Fairgrounds on the south side of Atlanta. At Lakewood in the winter of 1977 we saw many more prospective customers than the small country fairs had offered, but most were shopping for antiques or bargains. We began to understand the importance of finding appropriate markets for our products and began applying for juried spring craft shows.

Had Janice not helped me financially during this time of learning how to create and market gourdcrafts, I could never have gotten the business on its feet. I had drawn my teacher "retirement" of about $3,000 from the state of Georgia, and that was all the money I had to live on and buy gourds and supplies. Not only did Janice help to support me, but she also gave up many weekends to go to shows with me. When I look back on those times and think about them from her perspective, I'm amazed at her unselfishness, her faith, and her willing suspension of disbelief in the literal and figurative contents of our magic trunk.

gourd girls

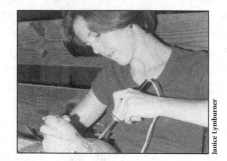

Janice Lymburner

Impersonating an Artist

*I*n the 1950s when I was in elementary school, our art program consisted of a smiling lady with big glasses and big arms who made a weekly visit to each classroom and handed out newsprint and crayons, enthusiastically instructing the children to "draw anything you want." I was the kind of kid who didn't know what to draw and therefore mostly produced boring square houses—the kind with a pointed roof, a door in the middle between two windows, and three lollipop flowers on each side of the house. That's who I was. No art teacher ever accused me of being creative or being able to draw. The only serious efforts I made to draw resulted from my childhood obsession with horses, and horses were a discouraging artistic subject for a little girl with eyes to see her work objectively.

Yet in the winter of 1977, despite my apparent lack of artistic talent, I decided to start embellishing the gourds. For this unlikely turn of events I credit my mother, who had always been multitalented as an artist, seamstress, and decorator. She had taught herself these skills and thus had taught me by example that the way to approach an artistic challenge was to bluff my way through until I knew what I was doing. So I must have taken for granted that I could learn to draw if that was what was required to make the gourd business succeed. My first experiences at shows had quickly shown me that most people didn't get as excited about the look of plain gourds as I did.

Woodburning—or gourd-burning—was my first means of decorating gourds. I bought a child's woodburning set and found that the tool wasn't hot enough to be effective on the hard shells of gourds. Then I graduated to a 40-watt soldering iron, which was hot enough but hard to control, especially on a smooth, rounded surface; so the point of the burner often slipped and hit my skin. Janice and I remember vividly the smell of burning flesh that became a part of our lives on winter nights when I worked on gourds and she graded school papers.

Before long I bought a Dremel tool, a small high-speed drill used by hobbyists, and began learning to carve designs into the surface of the gourds. Not only did the dimensionality of the designs fit the medium, but there was also a nice contrast in color and texture between the light, spongy inner surface of the gourd and the darker, smooth outer shell.

To increase the color contrast and also cover blemishes on many of the gourds, I began experimenting with ways to darken the outer shell. Eventually I tried leather dye and with it was able to achieve deep, natural-looking shades of brown, burnt orange, and burgundy, over which I applied varnish to seal the dye. We still use this combined technique of dyeing and carving gourds to make the containers and Christmas ornaments that became a staple of our business.

I never considered painting as a method of decorating the items I was making. I wanted a natural look and was convinced that a gourd as artistic material should be approached differently from a canvas. Though in recent years I have seen some beautiful painted gourds, I still maintain that these fruits are best decorated by methods that make use of their hollowness, their wood-like fiber, and the fact that they are three dimensional. My case is best made by world-renowned Peruvian and Nigerian gourd artists who for centuries have employed burning and carving as their primary techniques.

Wildflowers were an easy first choice of subject matter for my burned and carved designs. They held a fascination that had begun in the special place where Mildred, Janice, and I had met and learned to love life in the foothills of northeast Georgia. It was a Camp Fire Girls camp called Camp Toccoa, which still operates a few miles west of the town of Toccoa, about 25 miles from our present home in White County.

As a camp counselor I had found myself eye to eye with a magical

Janice Lymburner

Early gourd containers: left to right, *burned saxifrage design, carved hepatica, carved dogwood*

flower one evening while walking alone on a damp, seldom-used trail. This dime-sized flower, dangling from the branch of an evergreen shrub, was an elegantly crinkled white cup with delicate wine-colored embroidery inside. Eventually I learned the flower's identity: it was a mountain laurel bloom and had originally been part of a large cluster of identical flowers.

I was similarly awed a couple of years later while hiking on the Appalachian Trail near Wildcat Mountain in White County. A glowing white eight-petaled flower and the single delicate leaf that enfolded it had just emerged from the ground. The plant turned out to be a blood-root, known as one of the first flowers of spring in northeast Georgia. I made a decision then to open myself to a world of special friends, and wildflowers became a source of joy and comfort for me as well as pure evidence of the Life Spark moving on our planet.

So I began carving and burning wildflower designs on gourd containers. I spent hours in the woods making sketches that I later copied onto the gourds in chalk and then burned or carved. Practice, repetition, and love for native plants became my art teachers.

During this early period of trying to figure out what tools to use for decorating, cutting, and cleaning out the insides of gourds, I spent quite a bit of time wandering around Nix Hardware Store on the Cleveland square, looking at tools and thinking about possibilities. Watched curiously by male clerks who weren't used to having women—especially outlander women—haunting their store, I walked the creaky hardwood floors of Nix and breathed in its old-hardware-store smell, a combination of varnish, metal, and dust. I wanted to be free to look and think, but the clerks wanted to help me find things. They followed or watched me until I finally would buy something that wasn't what I really needed and leave.

Because of my discomfort I frequented the store less and less and began to fantasize about opening a hardware store for women. Eventually I discovered Habersham Hardware in the nearby town of Cornelia, where I could be a little more anonymous and where it wasn't long before a woman actually came to work in the tool department. The world was changing, but even today many visitors to our retail shop, The Gourd Place, still ask Janice, who manages it, "Does your husband do the cutting?" or "How does *he* cut the gourds?"

&

In March 1977, not long before we planted that first crop of gourds at Steve Smith's family farm, I participated in my first juried show, the Savannah Arts Festival. My parents, Bill and Betty Wilson, lived in Savannah at the time, so I was able to combine business with a visit to them. Because the show started on Friday, a school day, Janice was unable to make that trip with me.

I was painfully conscious that my parents and other relatives must have been concerned about me during that period. I was 26, was single with no boyfriend in sight, and had given up my teaching job to start a strange business in a rural area where I wasn't likely to meet eligible young men. I made no secret of my feminist convictions and used them as a kind of buffer against the subject of marriage. "Honey," my mother once asked me, "do you think you might get married someday if the ERA passes?" I shrugged awkwardly and changed the subject.

My maternal grandmother happened to be visiting my parents the weekend I was in Savannah for the arts festival. I remember her saying to me during that visit, "Well, Priscilla, you know there's a saying that

'Never was there a goose so gray that a gander didn't come her way.'"
If only she could have known how happy I was. Though Grandmama
always worried about my being an "old maid," she did share some of
my excitement about the business and always had helpful suggestions
for me. Having made a living as a seamstress and decorator from the
time her husband became ill at a young age, she was in large part the
source of the artistic know-how and inspiration that Mama passed on
to me.

Neither of my parents had a farming background or any particular
fondness for gourds. Like me, they probably had never thought about
gourds until 1976. Still, they tried to be supportive. I asked Daddy, who'd
always been a good carpenter, lots of questions about tools, and he tried
cutting a gourd with his electric jigsaw while I was there. I had been
cutting with a small hand saw that was frustrating and time-consum-
ing to use. The jig saw took only seconds, but the cut surface was quite
rough, so Daddy suggested that I try using a thin coping saw blade in
the saw rather than the thick blades designed for it.

When I got home I decided to invest $10 in an inexpensive Black
and Decker jigsaw. I removed the leveling platform from the bottom of
the saw for easier maneuverability and, using coping saw blades as Daddy
had suggested, was soon able to make smooth cuts that required no
sanding and allowed me to create containers with removable lids. This
advance remains the most important reason we've been able to make a
living working with gourds. My later discovery of a miniature jigsaw
allowed me to make even finer cuts.

Today gourd artists in the United States are numerous, and entire
catalogs of tools and supplies for gourdcrafting exist. Several companies
now manufacture miniature jigsaws partly because of the demand from
gourd artists. I could probably benefit from some of the tools on the
market but am reluctant to give up my own hard-earned methods.

❧

My need for raw material was growing, and I loved going on "gourd
hunts," as we called our trips to check out new sources. Janice liked to
go with me when she could. One of our all-time favorite gourd people
was Lou Westbrook of Crabapple, north of Atlanta. No doubt there's a
shopping strip now where we visited her modest, flowery, well-kept little farm. In August 1977, I wrote about her in my journal:

> J. and I met a neat lady the other day—Mrs. Westbrook.
> She grows gourds and flowers and all kinds of things.
> "Outdoors is what I like," she told us. "Outdoors. I like
> outdoors." I think she is like me in that she wants to do
> everything. At 73, she has a hard time accepting the fact
> that she can't do everything she wants to do. I hope I still
> feel this way when I'm her age.

The longest buying trip I made by myself that fall was to the home of a retired couple, Mr. and Mrs. W. S. B. North in Fort Valley, south of Macon. Though they lived right in town, Mr. North had a large garden spot in the backyard where he liked to grow gourds. I bought all 200 that he had and then couldn't seem to get away from this sweet white-haired couple. Mrs. North invited me to stay for a greasy hamburger lunch in their shaded old gray frame house, which smelled like the home of someone's grandparents. In that kitchen where we lunched, the year could have been 1947 instead of 1977.

I'd planned to make another stop on the way home in a little place called Arnoldsville, south of Athens. After following the directions I had received in a letter, I found myself standing at the front door of a huge, unpainted, dilapidated two-story house somewhere down a long dirt road off Georgia Highway 129. It could have been the home of "The Addams Family." I was afraid to knock. When I did, a woman of about 60 appeared who looked like a character from Carson McCullers' novel *Ballad of the Sad Café*. She introduced herself in a very formal, archaic way by pointing to herself and saying, "This is Katherine _____."

She proceeded to tell me in an equally convoluted way that I should in no way take advantage of her brother, Oscar, who had the gourds for sale. About that time Oscar, a short, bald, childlike man, joined her at the door. He was anxious to take me down to the basement and show me his gourds. I resisted a strong impulse to turn tail and run from the whole situation. With Katherine glaring after us from the top of the stairs, we descended to a dark basement, where Oscar proudly showed me his gourds, which numbered only about 12. They were small but very sturdy; I gladly bought them all and even more gladly headed for home.

I soon returned to the Athens area, this time to the town of Bogart, the home of another retired fellow who liked to garden. This man had placed an ad in the *Market Bulletin* offering 75 gourds to be given away; at the time I thought it worth the 150-mile drive round-trip to get the free gourds. When I arrived he showed me the gourds and helped me bag them up. As we carried the bags toward my VW bus, he stopped and said, "Come in my workshop for a minute. I want to show you something." We put down the bags and went inside his workshop, where he put his arms around me. His advances were easily rebuffed, but unnerving nonetheless. Then he insisted that he wanted to introduce me to his wife, who was playing bridge in their beautifully restored old house with her club.

The introduction must have been his way of trying to prove to me that he hadn't meant any harm. I received strange looks from the bridge ladies, who clearly had no use for gourds or hippie-looking young women. I made my exit as quickly as possible. Even the world of gourds could be strange and unpredictable; I was lucky that, as a young woman gallivanting around alone, I had no harm come to me.

Another trip to the Athens area around that period yielded not only a long-term gourd supplier, but also a friendship that still continues. A boy named Gary McLocklin, about 14 at the time, had grown several acres of gourds for his 4-H Club project with the help and support of his parents, Chester and Doris, and had advertised his gourds in the *Market Bulletin*. I bought several hundred gourds on that first visit to the McLocklin farm, which was located on a pretty stretch of Highway 82 between Statham and Bethlehem. The 4-H project was such a success that Gary continued growing gourds, and his parents continued and expanded the gourd-growing operation even after he grew up and went away to college.

My gourd-buying habit was necessary in that it supplied me with raw material and provided new artistic challenges as I discovered new shapes of gourds and puzzled over what to make from them. But I began to need more storage and workshop space than I had where we were still living, at the Nevilles' house in Cleveland. Moreover, Janice and I had begun wishing for a place of our own out in the country; it was time to make a difficult move.

gourd girls

Janice Lymburner

Finding Our Place

I had first moved in with Mildred and Janice three years earlier, in March of 1974. Hoping to find a teaching job in the northeast Georgia mountains, I had arranged to do my internship in Dahlonega, 20 miles west of Cleveland. The two of them had offered to let me stay with them for the spring quarter. We quickly became and looked like a threesome, all close to the same height and all with medium-length brown hair. We hiked together, attended a few concerts, and enjoyed eating out together at Cleveland's only two restaurants.

When my quarter of student teaching ended in May, I accepted a position for the fall in the English Department at Lumpkin County High School in Dahlonega. Mildred and Janice invited me to stay on with them. That summer Janice and I both found seasonal jobs at nearby Unicoi State Park, while Mildred's job as a psychologist with the Georgia Department of Corrections began to take her out of town frequently. Thus Janice and I began to spend more time together.

Janice was and is a smiling, beautiful person on the inside and the outside. Though she is blessed with pretty features, I believe she is also proof of the fact that inner beauty can reveal itself in a person's countenance. It is Janice's inner beauty that puts the sparkle in her blue eyes and the almost constant smile on her face, a blessing to all who experience it.

I knew deep down that I had fallen in love with her the first time I'd seen that smile in 1972. But it was during the spring and summer of 1974 that my feelings for her rose to a conscious level and would not be suppressed; likewise, Janice was struggling to make sense of her feelings for me.

Each of us wondered privately if there was any chance that our feelings could be mutual. Yet neither of us dared to speak what was in our hearts, both because mutuality seemed unlikely and because we assumed that same-gender relationships were wrong. I believed that telling Janice the truth about my feelings for her would mean the loss of her friendship. I spent many hours alone in the hayloft of the little barn behind our house, praying, crying, and trying to find the resolve to move out.

I couldn't seem to make a decision to leave. Finally on September 20, Janice and I found the courage to come out to ourselves and each other. Miraculously, the mutual feelings that we had been afraid to hope for were a reality. And in those first moments of facing the terrifying truth about ourselves, we were given a deep understanding that is as profound in its simplicity today as it was 30 years ago. The phrase we wonderingly repeated that day says what thousands of politicians and pundits, theologians and scholars cannot improve on, not in all their volumes of discourse: *This is love, and love cannot be wrong.* We recognized the goodness of love as surely as if we were holding it up in our hands and looking at it in all its radiance.

The monster I had been obsessively fearing and fleeing since my teenage years wasn't a monster at all. When I finally had the courage to look it full in the face, I saw that it was in reality a healthy part of me— my human need to love and be loved, to find the mate with whom I would share my life.

From that day on our lives were transformed. We were giddy with happiness, yet we had to cope with finding ourselves in the closet literally overnight. Although we never lost sight of the understanding that our love was not sick or morally wrong, we remained keenly aware of the way in which the world regarded same-gender love. In the mid-1970s only the most progressive psychologists were starting to recognize that homosexuality was not a mental illness. So, like millions of others before and after us, we kept the most important and sustaining fact of our lives a secret. For seven years we didn't consider telling Mildred or anyone else that we were a couple.

I had difficulty living with the fact that our relationship, had it been known to people, would have brought harsh disapproval. I became hypersensitive to the need for avoiding any look, any words that might betray the truth to people around us. Always tense, always on guard, I was especially fearful when we were with family members. Janice often asked me when we were alone again, "Is something wrong? You won't even *look* at me when we're with other people."

Four years older than me, Janice was more mature, more comfortable in her new skin, more able to be herself in spite of the closet; her leadership and integrity were powerful forces for me at that difficult stage in our relationship. Though the lie of omission was ever-present in our lives, we never lied aloud in the sense of making up boyfriend stories or laughing at jokes that ridiculed homosexuals.

We continued to live with Mildred for three more years, though as it happened, she moved into the upstairs apartment that was vacated a few months after Janice and I became a couple. She was also out of town more and more often with her job and other activities, so she became less a part of our old threesome by circumstance. We tried to pretend things were the same when she was with us, but I know Mildred must have felt inexplicably left out at times. Now I wish we had had the courage to explain the situation to her from the start.

In the fall of 1977 we began to make plans to move out, but we dreaded telling Mildred. Meanwhile, we spent time in the afternoons after school riding around White County in Janice's navy blue VW bug trying to find a house to rent. Like couples of all times and places, we were looking for our nesting spot.

One day in early October a teacher friend of Janice's mentioned that her uncle had a farmhouse for rent east of Cleveland on Blue Creek Road. After school that very day we rode out to see it. A solid-looking yellow-and-brown frame house with a big wrap-around porch, it sat back from the road in a yard that was, in the words of one of our favorite John Denver songs, "cool and green and shady." A large picture-book red barn stood 30 yards to the right of the house. Beyond it, a hundred acres of pasture land stretched all the way to the foot of Yonah, the same mountain we could see from the Nevilles' house in town. I still think of the Campbell farm as one of the most beautiful spots in a geographical area

View of Mount Yonah from the Campbells' pasture

John Kollock

where natural beauty is everywhere. The place felt right. As we stood in front of the house imagining ourselves as a farm family, a two-tone green truck with black cattle guards pulled into the driveway and a pleasant-looking couple in their 60s or 70s got out. The small man wore a fedora and walked with a limp that had been with him since polio had struck him in his prime.

"Hey there. I'm Clifford Campbell, and this is my wife Mildred." Mr. Campbell stuck out a firm hand in his trademark gesture and shook hands with each of us. We later learned that he had been Clerk of Court in White County for many years and was always politicking. He was known for the fact that he'd cross the street just to shake anyone's hand. "What can we do for you girls?"

Janice jumped right in to explain her connection. "I'm a teacher friend of your niece Joyce, and she was telling me this house might be for rent. I'm Janice Lymburner, and this is my friend Priscilla Wilson."

"Are you a teacher too?" Mrs. Campbell eyed me. She was a little taller and heavier-set than her husband. Both had gray hair, glasses, and easy manners.

"No, Ma'am, I was, but now I'm trying to get this—well, this gourd business going," I stumbled. "That's one reason we're looking for a place to rent in the country."

"Well, my Lord. What do you know about that?" She laughed a little to herself. "A gourd business."

"Yes, Ma'am, I make things out of gourds and decorate them."

"And it's just you two girls wantin' to live here right by yourselves?"

"Yes, Ma'am, just us."

We were always fearful when we met new people that they might guess our status as a couple. In retrospect, I realize that our youth made it easy for the Campbells to see us as roommates who would probably find men to marry before too long. I doubt if they even considered the possibility of our being a couple at that point, although many years later Mildred Campbell did refer obliquely to the fact that she had defended us—or at least our right to privacy—to some local folks.

"Well, I like the idea of renting to girls," I remember Mrs. Campbell saying. "I bet y'all would keep the place real nice." I breathed easier.

"Come on inside and see how you like it," said Mr. Campbell.

The front door opened into a small womb-like space where a piece of my heart still lives, a dimly lit room about 12 feet square that was wood on all six surfaces. The dark-stained horizontal pine boards on the walls were at least 15 inches wide; the floor and ceiling were identically stained narrower boards. There was a simple painted-brick fireplace on the wall opposite the front door.

To the right of the living room was a dining room of equal dimensions but with Sheetrock walls and ceiling. To the right of it was a small white-and-yellow kitchen with a few old-fashioned cabinets surrounding the chipped enamel sink, which looked out the front of the house toward the road. The kitchen smelled of mice, though I doubt if I recognized the smell at the time. A small storage room about 6 feet by 12 off the back of the kitchen had been created by enclosing a former back stoop; this room held potential gourd workshop space.

A hallway going straight back from the dining room led to two bedrooms and a small bath. The roomy bedroom on the left had several large windows and a long-unused fireplace that shared a chimney with the living room fireplace. The walls were painted bright pink. The smaller bedroom on the right was bright blue. Its only window, formerly to the outside, now looked out into the storage room.

The house had almost no closet space. The floors sagged, and the bedroom walls would need several coats of paint to cover the decorating tastes of the previous tenants. We loved it. The rooms would be difficult to heat with only the fireplaces and a couple of old unvented gas heaters, but this was a house that offered a different kind of warmth.

"You girls would have to keep the place mowed," said Mrs. Campbell as we walked back outside. "Could you do that?"

"Yes, Ma'am, we could get a mower," we assured her.

Today, no matter how right a choice feels to me, I need to sleep on it. Back then decisions seemed less weighty. Mr. Campbell offered us the place for $75 a month, and we took it on the spot.

We went home and faced the task of telling Mildred our plans, emphasizing the need for gourd storage space as the reason for our move. Much to our relief, she took the news in stride and was happy for us. We had a place in the country and our best friend's blessing.

John Kollock

Life Is Good

*I*n the weeks that followed I spent much of my time putting coat after coat of ivory paint on the bedroom walls while Janice taught school. I was 27, still young enough to enjoy painting. My parents, always ready for a decorating project—especially to help one of their children—came from Savannah to our aid, pulling my childhood piano and Mama's sewing machine in a U-Haul trailer. Mama made simple muslin curtains for the many large windows in the house while Daddy put plastic over the windows to keep out drafts.

Janice's mother, Nancy Lymburner, lived and worked in Atlanta and was unable to spend much time with us during that period, but she came to see the house—and loved it as much as we did. Always an independent and adventurous spirit herself, she had been a strong supporter of the gourd business from the start.

By the end of October we had moved into the farmhouse that became our home for the next nine good years. Our relationship with each other, though unknown to any other person, was happy and solid. We began nesting together in earnest, enjoying the ordinary daily tasks of living as well as the task of furnishing our cozy but drafty home.

Always conscious of a mutual distaste for role-playing, we worked out a division of labor that allowed each of us to have both boy-jobs and girl-jobs. Janice took on most of the cleaning and laundry responsibilities as well as lawn care, while I became the handy-woman and learned to cook. Unaware of that bad word *cholesterol*, I made Janice's favorite food, fried chicken, at the drop of a hat and also enjoyed learning to make bread and can some of the vegetables we grew.

It was our privilege during that time to play at farm life, living a scaled-down, user-friendly version of *Forty Acres and Independence*. With the indulgence of the Campbells, we raised a pig; three pet calves in need of special care, one of which we once took to the vet in the back seat of Janice's Toyota; two goats; and several guineas. We had heard an old saying from craft show spectators: "gourds, goats, and guineas go together; they're all useless." So naturally we had to have all three.

There were several wild game hens living on the place when we first arrived, and we had the thrill of searching for their delicious eggs in the large, hay-filled, dusty barn. I began to enjoy eggs for the first time in my life. We grew our first vegetable gardens in a small but very rich spot in the front yard but were advised that we shouldn't work in the garden—or mow the grass—on Sundays because we would be visible to disapproving passers-by. We read Ruth Stout's book *Gardening Without Work* and became true believers in her radical mulch method of gardening, enjoying much greater success as vegetable gardeners than we ever would as gourd farmers. We even sent her one of our gourd containers as an appreciation gift.

On weekends Janice sometimes helped me clean gourds in the grassy side yard where we soaked them in a child's wading pool. We enjoyed telling people, "Oh, dahling, we spent the loveliest afternoon out by the pool!" It wasn't long before we began paying other people to clean the gourds, but in those early days at the Campbell farm we didn't mind doing it.

We took long daily walks in the pasture, which measured almost a mile deep from the highway entrance back to the foot of Yonah Mountain. Now that we lived almost in the shadow of its wooded side, Yonah felt like a benevolent guardian rather than the stern, rock-faced icon we had seen from our home in Cleveland.

During our walks we enjoyed watching the Campbells' 40 or 50 cows at close range. Like silly children, we gave them names and teased them verbally to their utter disregard. We played games of "redlight" with them in which they had only to do what cows do best, stand and stare, while we

John Kollock

Janice and Priscilla relaxing by the pool

ran away from them to the count of 10 and turned to see if they had moved.

Particularly in the winter their stillness fascinated me. One night I wrote the following in my journal:

> What I'd like to remember about this past month is the way the cows are still and quiet—the whole world, for that matter—on cold, cold winter days. I couldn't help remarking several times that they looked like statues. We watched the whole group of 50 or so standing around in the pasture for several minutes without seeing one of them move.

Once during calving season, February or March, we saw a fat cow lying down, and we were convinced that she was about to give birth. Never having seen such an event before, we decided to watch in hopes of getting lucky. We sat down on the ground about 30 feet away from the cow and waited. Maybe half an hour passed before she finally started to make a little noise and struggle to her feet.

"Do they have their calves standing up?"

"I think so. This may be it!"

Some part of her rear end opened up. We watched in rapt excitement as a big load of poop came out. We had a long way to go before we could call ourselves country folks.

Not long after Janice and I moved to the farm there was a knock at our door one evening. The tall, awkward elderly man who stood there simply announced his name in a very deep voice: "John Head." I had heard the Campbells speak of him as their friend, so I invited him inside.

He had heard that we needed firewood, and he wanted to come to our aid. In his view we were helpless women in need with winter bearing down on us. There was always a great gap between Mr. Head's perception and our own of just how helpless we were; the truth was somewhere in the middle. But his desire to be of help was the reason our friendship began.

A widower with no children, Mr. Head was retired and had time on his hands. "I'm going to do *something*, even if it's wrong!" he'd thunder. Thus he insisted time after time on helping us with a variety of projects. He helped us get firewood (his old jeep, "Nellie Belle," could go anywhere), make kraut, can beans, and, of course, attempt to grow gourds.

Mr. Head had spent most of his life in White County. Gardening and raising livestock were a way of life for him, and yet he took as much pleasure in them as any novice. Every year he raised a hog, and he loved to speculate about how much each one weighed or how long it was. One fall he and Janice had a bet going about whether his hog was as long as our sofa. They never agreed on who won the bet, though, because he maintained that the hog's tail counted in the measurement, while Janice never would concede that point.

One year a few of the Campbells' friends and relatives decided to raise hogs together at the farm, and they offered to let us in on the project. There were about six or eight hogs in the small pasture adjoining the barn; fortunately, we didn't know which one was ours and tried not to get attached to any of them.

Killing day came, and Janice and I stayed inside on that cold November morning while John Moss, whose business was killing, dehairing, and quartering hogs, shot the animals and took them away. Mr. Head had made arrangements to pick up our hog along with his own from Mr. Moss' place later that day and transport them to his small white frame house in Cleveland, where we would "work them up" together outside on a makeshift table of sawhorses and plywood. He guided us through the process of cutting up the meat into roasts, pork chops, and buckets of scrap pieces that would become sausage. I'll never forget the feeling of that still-warm meat in my bare hands.

Periodically Mr. Head sharpened our long knives with old-fashioned tools he had inherited from his parents. As we worked he helped to distract us from our queasiness by explaining the process of curing hams and "rendering lard" to make chitlins and by telling us stories from his childhood about community hog-killing days. He never told us a story related to us later by the Campbells: his father had been killed by hogs when, as an old man, he had fallen into their pen.

Mr. Head—he wanted us to call him "John," but we never did—was like a kid every spring about starting his garden. He always planted too early, even though he knew better. Most years he'd have to replant, but there were times when he was the first to have beans and tomatoes. Never much of a vegetable eater himself, he loved to give away his produce. "Why, you're just as welcome to it as the air you breathe," he'd say, handing us grocery bags overflowing with vegetables we didn't want but didn't have the heart to refuse.

What he couldn't give away he canned or froze. In the summer he bragged about the number of cans and freezer bags he had put up, only to start complaining the next winter that if his friends didn't help him use the food he'd have to "th'ow it in the brainch." He gave us literally cases of beans, kraut, pickled corn, and canned sausage. He had two freezers in his basement and two on his porch, all full of meat and vegetables he had put up. His dining room had become a warehouse for canned goods. "I know people think I'm foolish," he'd say, "but, by God, I've got to keep busy doing something."

Mr. Head loved to "fool wi' coon dogs." He always had several in a smelly pen near his house, and almost every time I talked to him on the phone he was in the process of buying or selling another one. Each deal was the deal of a lifetime. I usually asked him, just to make conversation, what the new dog's name was; he'd pause for several seconds and then say, in his deep voice, "Queen." I'm not sure if he actually named all the dogs "Queen" or if he just told me the first name that came to mind. He couldn't have explained to the likes of me how a person can feel affection and appreciation for a coon dog without giving it a name. He did often yell, "Queen!" to the whole pack of them from his porch to quiet them down.

One of the things I began noticing about our new local friends during the years at the Campbell farm was how extravagant they were in their praise of people they liked or admired. Any time Mr. Head wanted to give someone a great compliment, he described them as "always the same, never in a hurry." Though Janice and I cared for and appreciated Mr. Head, we kept our defenses up against the constant presence that he wanted to be in our lives. No doubt we seemed changeable and in a hurry at times. Living in the closet makes one fiercely and painfully protective of the small private space inside.

One night Mr. Head phoned and said to me in a deep, mysterious voice, "Prisciller, you girls need to know that folks around here are a-talkin' about you."

My heart racing, I finally managed to say, "I don't know what you mean." My words came out with a cold finality that ended the conversation before it started. He received neither the reassurance of our "innocence" that he'd hoped for nor confirmation of the rumors.

"Well, okay, bye," was his awkward response. We didn't see him for a week or two, and then he showed up on our front porch once again with a grocery sack full of vegetables, acting as if the exchange had never taken place.

Red Clay and Credibility

One evening during our first winter at the Campbell farm, I had a phone call from my former principal at nearby Lumpkin County High School. He needed an English teacher in the middle of the year and was offering me my job back. It was a moment of truth for me. My brief teaching career passed before my eyes as I considered the offer.

Unlike Janice, who had always known she wanted to be a teacher, I had never been drawn to that profession. As a small child I had wanted to be a clown or a horse jockey, but I'd consistently drawn a blank as I grew older. The list of women's occupations had been short and uninteresting to me: teacher, nurse, dental hygienist, telephone operator, airline stewardess. "Gourd girl" was nowhere on the list. I had majored in English at Auburn University and had never become clear about career goals.

In September 1974, the same month that Janice and I became a couple, I had begun teaching high school English by default. I'd enjoyed getting to know the students, but as a young and ostensibly single teacher had been the object of their curiosity about my love life. The truth of my love for Janice, which I guarded with all my strength, felt like it was written all over my face. Some of the students were amazingly perceptive and made remarks to me such as, "Ooooh, Miss Wilson, I can just tell you're in love. Is he anybody we know? Aren't you going to tell us who he is?" I well remember how frightened I felt as I evaded their questions, pretending to be coy.

I lived with a pounding headache. I was unable to relate to my students comfortably and didn't attend after school events as a high school teacher should, so my career as a teacher was doomed from the start. As I have said, I didn't renew my contract after the second year of teaching.

I'll never know whether I'd have been a good teacher without the handicap of the closet. I turned down the second chance offered me that winter night in 1978 and, true to my ambivalent nature, immediately wondered if I had done the wrong thing. Alone in my little workshop every day while Janice was at school, I struggled with worries about whether the gourd business could support me. Mount Yonah and the pasture land behind our house beckoned me, and I spent more time wandering there than I liked Janice to know.

One warm February afternoon when I was feeling particularly lost, I sought comfort in a friendly old mulberry tree with low branches spreading wide. After sitting in the tree for a while, I felt a strange idea bubbling up inside me as if alive: I wanted to make a likeness of the earth from a gourd. This gourd globe would allow people to see the earth as it looks without countries or borders. I wasn't aware at the time that round gourds existed or that creation myths of several different cultures had likened our planet to a gourd.

I describe the strange birth of the globe idea not to give it undue significance but to acknowledge and give thanks for the saving grace that the Creative Force has been for me and others in our inner lives. Time and again unlikely ideas from the universe have found me, rescued me from obsessive worry, and placed me squarely in the present with an enticing task before me.

Janice was as captivated as I was by the idea. Though the globe did not come into being until a year later, it stayed very much in our consciousness. We even toyed with the idea of changing the name of our business to Gourd Earth Products—a name that, though roundly rejected by friends at the time, foreshadowed another gift from the universe that would come 22 years later.

&

As the winter of 1978 progressed, Janice and I talked about finding a gourd field to rent close to our new home in Blue Creek. Mr. Head knew of a seven-acre field four miles from us that Chester and Clara Dalton in the Union Grove Community had for rent. In fact, he had lived in that part of the county as a child and had helped his family grow cotton on the piece of land in question. He assured us that it was a rich field, though he thought the rent of $15 an acre per year was exorbitant.

I made an appointment with the Daltons and went to see them one very cold morning after Janice left for school. Nervous about how I, an outlander and a woman, would be received, I summoned my courage and knocked on their door. Clara, a small, serious white-haired woman in a cotton house dress and two tired cardigan sweaters, invited me into the modest old white frame farmhouse and led me through a dark hallway to the small living room where Chester waited. He was a stocky man in bib overalls with plenty of wrinkles in his broad tanned face but not a gray hair among the black ones on his head.

Mr. Head in front of his jeep "Nellie Belle"

The three of us sat in straight wooden chairs in front of their high brick hearth where a small fire powerfully contradicted the idea that fireplaces don't give heat. I can still see that fire and feel its warmth. Chester, Clara, and I tried to communicate in the way that people do when they want to convey feelings of goodwill but don't quite speak the same language. They must have been mystified at the idea of two young women wanting to grow seven acres of anything, much less gourds. But the smile pushing its way onto Chester's wide face told me he couldn't help feeling a little excitement. He had planted a few gourds for purple martin birdhouses the previous spring and had been pleased with his crop. Besides, they did want renters, and they let me know they respected the fact that I was eager to learn. We struck a deal.

The plot of ground we would be renting, which looked like several football fields compared to the previous year's plot, was on a gently sloping hillside 50 yards or so above and to the right of the house. As Chester and I walked toward the terraced field, he showed me his small, now-frozen gourd patch nearby. Plump, frosty gourds practically covered the ground. Chester told me with a sly grin and much relish, as if he were tasting his words, how he had kept the patch clean of weeds by pulling the dirt around the vines with the cultivators on his Farmall H tractor—a large, ancient-looking, rusty-red machine I had seen parked in the driveway.

Now I think I understand a little of what Chester was saying and feeling; I've earned my own good memories of the beauty of machinery doing a job properly and efficiently, and I can see in my own mind's eye the lovely motion of fine reddish-brown dirt flowing over weed sprouts. At the time I understood little except his deep love of growing things and was moved by that alone.

In the weeks that followed, Mr. Head and Janice and I excitedly made plans for the new crop—how many rows we could fit on each terrace of the big field, what kinds of gourds we'd plant on each, how much fertilizer we would need. Mr. Head insisted that Rainbow "fertilize," as he called it, was the best. We still buy that brand for no other reason than his belief in its magic.

As spring approached and our anticipation grew, Janice asked Mr. Head how we would know when the time was right for planting. "Well, I'll tell you what. My grandpa knew a Cherokee feller, and he said that the time to plant corn—hit'd be the same for gourds—was as soon as the white oak leaves were as big as a mouse's ear. I always think of that at plantin' time."

The reality, among other hard truths that we learned about farming and life during that time, was that even after temperatures were warm enough as indicated by the foliage on the trees, you simply couldn't plow and plant until the ground was ready. The soil had to be moderately dry to a depth of 8 to 12 inches before it could be turned or harrowed. Otherwise the wet chunks of dirt would turn into bricks that could prevent seeds from germinating and plague the farmer the entire season.

There was nothing a human being could do to speed the drying process after a spring rain. Year after year we had to wait patiently and faithfully, knowing that unless gourd vines were planted by early May the fruits would not have time to mature on the vine and would be useless. Immature gourds rot instead of becoming woody and permanent.

When April arrived and the ground was finally dry enough, a friend of Mr. Head's plowed the field for us. Even with the help of Mr. Head, Mildred Neville, and our friends who had helped the previous year, it took days and days to plant the entire seven acres by hand. By the time Janice, Mr. Head, and I finished the job, the weeds were already coming up; and by the time the gourds sprouted three long weeks later, billions more were thriving on Rainbow fertilizer. Morning glories, nut grass, and cockleburs quickly became important enough in our lives that we added their names to the list of weeds we'd learned about the previous year.

We saw less and less of Clara and Chester as the spring wore on. I don't think they could stand to look at the field that under their care had no doubt been a picture postcard of lush green corn stalks. The last time I remember seeing them at the field they both shook their heads sadly and said again and again, "You're lettin' 'em [the weeds] get away from you."

I hoed, waking and sleeping. Janice assisted when she could, and Mr. Head wanted to help; but I couldn't accept his help day after day. So I was alone many hours with the struggling gourd vines, the weeds, the red dirt, and the sun. I saw cockleburs, waking and sleeping. My aching legs seemed to be dyed a red clay color, as were all my ruined socks and shoes.

It happened that Mildred had completed an Outward Bound survival course around that time, and I remember creating a sarcastic spoof of such programs in my mind as I hoed. I called my program "Westward Hoe." The brochure would exhort prospective participants to "develop your strength and character as you hoe row after row of gourd vines in the scalding sun. Find out the true meaning of that time-honored phrase about a 'long row to hoe.' Test your survival skills as you battle cockleburs to the death!" My perspective on recreation and labor, for better and for worse, began to resemble that of a practical-minded country person who values productivity and pragmatism above all else.

Sometime during the winter and spring of that year, Janice and I made the decision that she would become a full-time partner in the business. Gourdcraft Originals was doing well by our modest standards, and after eight years of teaching, Janice was ready for a change. The decision didn't seem difficult or earthshaking at the time; she simply did not renew her teaching contract that spring.

In retrospect, it was a more serious and important decision than we realized—as my decision to leave teaching had been. Already living on the edge socially as closeted lesbians, we now began living on the edge financially as well. Twenty-five years later, we think about the retirement incomes we'd now have awaiting us if we'd both stayed in teaching. But then we think of the unique opportunities our business has afforded us, not the least of which was the freedom to come out of the closet when we were finally ready in the early 1990s. Retirement or no retirement, we still grin in the mornings when we hear the school bus go by our house.

When school was out, Janice and I continued facing the weeds together. It was clear that what we needed—in addition to experience and good sense—was a tractor. Mr. Head valiantly offered to hook up a "gee-whiz," a kind of spring-toothed harrow, behind his old jeep, Nellie Belle, but he made only three or four swipes through the field with the rig before the rusted gee-whiz broke under the strain.

Next we managed to convince a tractor dealer in nearby Gainesville to haul one of his machines to our field so we could try it out. We admitted to the man that we probably couldn't really afford to buy a tractor, but he must have thought we were cute and felt sorry for us. At any rate, he brought out a shiny orange Kubota and let us use it—until I ran it out of gas and couldn't get it started again without knowing how to prime the fuel pump.

In desperation we introduced ourselves to the Daltons' neighbor, Johnny Seegers, and begged him to plow for us with his tractor. Johnny, a smiling, clean-cut guy of medium build with dark brown hair and horn-rimmed glasses, looked more like a businessman than a gardener. "I don't hire out," he told us. He was soft-spoken but firm.

The next afternoon we arrived to find him harrowing the "middles," or spaces between rows, with cutting harrows behind his red International Harvester. We gratefully promised not to tell anyone he had done the work. Even though he would not accept payment and therefore had not "hired out," he didn't want to be associated in any way with the disaster area we were calling a gourd field. It was a matter of pride for Johnny, whose own garden and person were immaculate.

Even though Johnny wiped out billions of weeds with his tractor, there were billions more that were too close to the struggling gourd vines to be dug safely with harrows. We hoed for dear life. After the weeds got to be thigh-high we gave up on hoeing and began sling-blading just to buy time. Waking and sleeping, we fought the cockleburs.

When a *real* farmer grows gourds, he or she usually "lays 'em by" six or eight weeks into the growing season after the vines have begun to cover the ground and cannot be cultivated any longer. But for us, as in the previous year, laying-by time never came. We gradually gave up the fight, hoped for the best, and turned our attention to producing gourdcrafts for fall shows.

During the spring of 1978 just before planting time, I exhibited in a craft show at Lenox Square in Atlanta and attracted the attention of a display designer from Neiman-Marcus department store. She ordered 28 large decorated gourd containers with assorted wildflower designs. I worked on the containers throughout the spring between hoeing sessions and had them ready for delivery about the time we gave up on the gourd field in late June.

Janice and I saw this order as an important break in that it gave my work a little of the credibility we craved with friends and family members. We excitedly delivered the gourds on the first of July and went back to Neiman's a few weeks later to see and photograph the finished displays. Our gourds looked fine, spotlighted and draped with jewelry in elegant display cases. As we stood admiring them and feeling good about our prospects, we were light years away from the dusty, weedy gourd field where we had stood only a day or two before.

Gourd with a burned ox-eye daisy design in the Neiman-Marcus display

Janice Lymburner

passed by our booths was seeing gourds as a craft medium for the first time. Many were enthusiastic and complimentary, but some people tried to cleverly sum up the whole craft form with one terse question: "Whadda-ya do, shellac 'em?" The question irritated us at first and then began to make us laugh as we heard it more and more often.

Some people were quite open about the fact that they wanted to copy our ideas. Others stood back at a distance, eyeing our work, taking pictures, and talking softly to each other. "I've got some gourds in my barn," we often heard people say. "I'm going to do this." If every person who went home and tried gourdcrafting had paid us a dollar, we would be wealthy today.

🐜

We were still buying gourds from various farmers around Georgia, having grown few useful ones in our first effort. Like craft fairs, gourd hunts were more fun than ever now that the two of us could go together. Janice teased me and still does about how excited I can get over going to see a new batch of gourds. We went into chicken houses, barns, and outbuildings of every description, many of which were mouse-infested, dangerously deteriorating, or filthy with ancient dust. We went on several wild-goose chases, driving hours and hours to such places as Harpersville, Alabama or Unadilla, Georgia, where we didn't even find desirable gourds. Janice humored me endlessly and smilingly.

Gourds were cheap in the old days—usually only 50 cents each wholesale—and sometimes we got even better deals by taking all that a farmer had for sale, even though some in the lot were not the shapes we wanted. So we began to accumulate many gourds that weren't the right shapes for containers, planters, matchstick holders, and other production items we were making.

Periodically I would take out some of these odd-shaped fruits and stare at them, wondering what to do with them. One day as I looked at a gourd that was shaped like an elephant without legs, something clicked. All I had to do was give the elephant some wheels, and it would have a reason for being as well as the ability to stand up on its own four "feet." Turtles, snails, whales, and aardvarks quickly followed.

Soon we had a menagerie of animals that served an important purpose in our development—they started us on the road to whimsy and to a different way of perceiving the possibilities represented by a gourd. I

Priscilla and Janice, wearing gourd name tags, displaying gourds on wheels at the Savannah Arts Festival

began to distinguish in my mind between two artistic concepts I was employing: one in which a gourd was an object to decorate and put to some ostensible use, and one in which a gourd *became* something else altogether, creating an illusion of sorts. When I gave that first elephant gourd toy its wheels, eyes, ears, and tail, it *became* an elephant. As a would-be clown since childhood, I loved the idea of creating illusions.

John Kollock

Growing Friendships

$\mathcal{B}$ack in our gourd field at the Daltons', the sheer number of vines we had planted ensured that we would get *something* for our labors, and we did have a better crop than the previous year—about 500 respectable-sized gourds. We decided to have a harvest party and invited 20 friends to have fun on a cold day in January trampling through a field of tall dead weeds searching for gourds.

Several people brought vehicles for transporting the gourds, including Mr. Head, who brought Nellie Belle. The small truck bed on the back of the jeep didn't hold many gourds, but Nellie Belle could drive all over the field without getting stuck.

Mildred's dad, Rae Neville, brought his 1950 Chevrolet. The truck had been shiny red in its glory days, but now it was two shades of dull gray and had a small bed with gray wooden sides to increase its capacity. Mildred and her dad insisted on the old truck's participation even after larger trucks were being pressed into service; both Mr. Neville and the truck became icons throughout the years of gourd gatherings. Mr. Neville, who was in his 80s, was a short but sturdy man with a cute smile and flyaway white hair that attracted dozens of cockleburs when he bent down to pick up gourds in the field. People took turns during the day trying to remove the cockleburs, but as soon as he re-entered the field he had a head-full again.

Mr. Neville with a head full of cockleburs

John Kollock

John Kollock

Lona Smith helps gather gourds

The party was a great success and turned out to be the beginning of a tradition that lasted for the dozen or so years that we continued to grow gourds. We always were better at growing friendships than growing gourds. For those first gatherers Janice and I provided lunch, which consisted of homemade bread, soup, and fruit; a supper of pork roast, two salads, and pineapple souffle; and even gourd T-shirts as favors. The shirts bore a design I had created showing a gourd as the earth with subtle markings suggesting continents. I don't think many people realized the gourd was supposed to represent the earth, but Janice and I took pleasure in that secret.

It wasn't long after the harvest until the mice discovered our small crop of gourds stored in one of the sheds at the Campbell farm. We were horrified when we saw our hard-earned crop being destroyed as the rodents chewed through the shells to gain access to the seed. We immediately began putting out poison, which seemingly wasn't as tasty as the gourd seed. Next we tried one of those electronic gadgets that emits a high-pitched sound guaranteed to drive rodents away; still no luck.

Finally Mrs. Campbell stated the obvious: "You girls are just gonna have to get you some cats." Though neither Janice nor I had been "cat people" up to this time, we now took in several that became enthusiastic gourd guards. As usual, the country folks' remedy made sense—and made us many feline friends over the years.

In February of 1979, not long after the gourd gathering, our first short television feature was aired. Somehow Atlanta newscaster Phil Flynn and then-cameraman Leroy Powell had heard about the gathering and had come the week before the event to tape one of their "Georgia Camera" installments. Janice and I sounded predictably amateurish in the interviews, but we were thrilled with the publicity. We still craved the credibility that, for better or for worse, television coverage lends to its chosen subjects. Mildred, ever our strongest supporter, took pictures of Leroy and Phil at work and submitted an article to the *White County News* about our television debut.

We thought we had arrived; we didn't yet understand that living the gourd life means never getting there but staying engaged in the journey.

One cold, damp winter night in 1979, around the time of the mouse infestation, we had a phone call from Ruth Stovall Head, who turned out to be a neighbor. In Blue Creek, the term "neighbor" might include anyone who lives within an area of perhaps six or eight square miles, but its use is primarily limited to those for whom one has an affinity. Not only did we quickly feel an affinity for Mrs. Head, but she became our guide to the history and character of Blue Creek.

She didn't identify herself when I answered the phone but just started talking in her twangy voice, part city and part country. "I hear you girls are a'lookin' for some farmland to rent."

Before I could say anything, another conversation erupted on the party line. "Lilianne, are you on the line? Lilianne, I know you're there. Hang up, please."

"I'm a-needin' to use the phone, Ruth."

"Well, you'll have to wait your turn. Now hang up, please."

I was on the phone with two old ladies, neither of whom I knew. Janice and I later learned that Ruth Stovall Head and Lilianne Satterfield had been rivals for the use of the same party line for years. Lilianne stayed on the line in silence even though Mrs. Head kept letting her know in a snappy voice that she didn't appreciate the intrusion. "All right," she'd say, or "Yes, we'll see about this" or "I know what you're up to." For me the conversation was very confusing, because I wasn't always sure which of us Mrs. Head was addressing or when I should speak.

Mrs. Head, who was not related to our friend John Head, eventually communicated to me who she was and where she lived—just a little over a mile from us. She had several different farm fields for rent on the Stovall family farm, and Janice and I were once again in the market. Clara and Chester Dalton, our previous landlords, could not have stood the humiliation of having their farmland grow up in tall weeds another summer as it had under our care.

I agreed that we would come and take a look at the Stovall fields. Thanks to Lilianne, our plans were no doubt known to everyone in Blue Creek within a few hours.

The next afternoon Janice and I drove a mile north on Blue Creek Road and turned right into the shady, inviting dirt lane that led to Mrs. Head's house. As we rounded the last curve and saw the Stovall home place for the first time, we felt as though we were entering the pages of a storybook. An impressive old two-story white frame house sat on a hill above the road to our right; to our left beside Blue Creek, which was as wide as a small river at that point, stood a weathered but sturdy old mill. Ahead of us was a wooden bridge and, beyond it, a picturesque old unpainted barn. We later learned that the Stovall farm had once been the center of the Blue Creek community. In addition to the buildings we now admired, there had been a cover over the wooden bridge and a store—the "storehouse," Mrs. Head called it—next to the mill.

Ruth Head was outside sweeping the dirt area in front of the porch when we drove up. She was a short, slender woman, probably in her early 70s at that time, with a heavy brace on one leg. Her medium-length dark hair—with almost no gray in it—looked as though it had just been shampooed and set, and the flower-print blouse she wore with her jeans was crisp and spotless. We introduced ourselves and sat down on her porch to get acquainted. She had a sweet face and demeanor but was quite reserved—almost stern—in her way of relating to us.

"Now tell me, are you girls sisters or not? Lots of people around here call you the gourd sisters," she started out. We'd been asked the question before and knew that some folks dealt with their uneasiness about the nature of our relationship by thinking of us as sisters. They wanted to like us and unconsciously felt better about our living and working together if we were related by blood.

"No, Ma'am, we're just friends," we said.

"Well, I'll call you the gourd girls, then," she pronounced, and much to our relief proceeded to tell us her own story. She had grown up in the house where we were now sitting and married a local man who all too quickly broke her heart. After her divorce she moved to Atlanta, where for many years she worked in the children's apparel department at the downtown Davison's department store. After her retirement she returned to Blue Creek to care for her childhood home and 150-acre farm.

Mrs. Head—though she came to like us very much, she never did invite us to call her Ruth—was exceedingly proud of the home place and fiercely protective of it. Often she would make disparaging remarks about one local developer in particular who in her opinion wanted to turn the Stovall property into a subdivision someday. At that time a few subdivisions were beginning to spring up in the historically rural area, and Mrs. Head saw the handwriting on the wall. She despised the idea of houses being built near her farm on lots of "nothing but one little acre," believing that these houses would attract "the wrong kind of people."

Seeing that we were sympathetic with her concerns about her family property, our prospective landlady seemed satisfied with us and offered to show us the farmland for rent. There were four fields ranging in size from half an acre to a couple of acres. One of the fields had a fine view of Mount Yonah, and two were in sight of a log cabin built in the 1800s by Mrs. Head's aunt and uncle. I felt as though we had stepped even further into the storybook past.

Ruth Head reminisced at length that day and on other occasions about life on the farm when she was a child: about the camaraderie her family had shared with the Tatums, their closest neighbors; about farm activities such as pulling fodder; about the important role her father's mill and storehouse had played in the community. Much to my fascination, she used many almost-forgotten words such as *gew-anner* (guano), *terrapin*, and *brogans*. So vivid were her descriptions and so alive was she as she talked that she made me nostalgic for a time in history I'd never known. I still vicariously experience her longing for the old days.

Finally we had found our place to farm. Janice and I enjoyed and coveted the Stovall farm from that day forth for several years. We were privileged to know it before, just as Mrs. Head predicted, housing developments and resorts surrounded and invaded it, obscuring its old magic.

Mrs. Head became one of our biggest supporters, never doubting our ability to succeed as farmers. Unlike some local people, she took us seriously and seemed to think it was perfectly natural for two women to be growing acres of gourds. I believe she saw us as strong, independent women like herself. In fact, she came to regard us as peers, often forgetting that we were young enough to be her grandchildren. As she lamented modern society's ills, she often said to us endearingly, "Now, when *we* were girls, things were different!"

Even as such remarks betrayed the senility beginning to creep over her, Mrs. Head maintained her competence as a gardener. Her love of plants was second only to her love of the farm itself. Childless and alone most of her adult life, in retirement she lavished her affection on foxgloves and pinks and coreopsis growing on the bank in front of her house; she gave her tenderness to the corn, squash, and bean seedlings she planted each year in her "storehouse garden," exactly where the much-grieved general store had stood beside Blue Creek before it burned down. In spite of the brace on one leg, she worked in the yard most of her waking hours. When her garden vegetables were young, she struggled to carry buckets of water from the creek for them as though they were small children whose lives depended on her.

As summers wore on and droughts set in, Mrs. Head often said to us in all earnestness, "Girls, let's pray for a big dew!" She was a living example of the fact that gardening can keep a person young and hopeful for a lifetime. I believe Janice and I both absorbed some of her reverence for growing things.

gourd girls

John Kollock

The Kindness of Strangers

*A*round the same time we found the Stovall place, we decided we had to have a tractor—even though the idea of such an expenditure was intimidating. We pored over the farm equipment section of the *Farmers and Consumers Market Bulletin* every week, looking for a good deal on an old Farmall Cub or Ford 8-N.

Then one afternoon as we were driving the back way home from nearby Gainesville to Cleveland, we spotted a strange-looking machine for sale in the front yard of a gray clapboard house. It looked like an orange dune buggy. Janice jammed on the brakes of F. R. Chick, our old white Toyota Corolla—so named because it had smelled like fried chicken, Janice's very favorite food, when it was new.

We pulled into the driveway, got out, and stood staring at the adorable piece of machinery.

M. J. Hollifield, the tractor's owner, came out of the house. He was a heavy-set guy with curly gray hair and a friendly face. "You two ladies looking for a tractor?"

"Yeah, what kind is this?" Janice asked.

"Why, this is the dandiest little tractor ever made—a 1952 G model Allis Chalmers. It may be small, but it's got 26 horsepower. What makes this tractor different from most is that some of the cultivators go near the

John Kollock

Priscilla planting gourds at the Stovall farm

front, right up under you. When you're plowing, you can look straight down and see your row, make sure you're not covering up your plants! Do you girls grow a big garden?"

As we took turns sitting on the seat, we told him about our gourd business. He was obviously amused, but he took our need for a tractor seriously. He showed us how the manual lifts worked—one on the front and one on the back—and let us try them to see if we had enough strength to raise and lower the bars on which the cultivators were individually mounted. Like many machines of its kind and vintage, this one had no hydraulic lift. Neither of us minded; we were young, strong, and in love with a tractor. We bought Tiny T, as Janice quickly dubbed it, for $1,650, including six cultivators and delivery.

Though we were thrilled with our new toy, we knew better than to think Tiny T was capable of preparing five acres of ground for planting. When April came, we began the difficult task of finding someone with a large tractor to plow the Stovall fields for us.

For weeks we harangued several neighbors with our desperate pleas, but no one seemed to want the job. Finally someone suggested that we try Rev. Leon Carter, who still lives on Blue Creek Road with his wife, Mary.

I reached Mary on the phone one evening, explained our plight, and waited to be turned down once again. I can still remember her friendly response: "The Stovall farm? Why that's just a hop, skip, and a jump from us. Leon can probably get over there in a day or two. I'll talk to him about it." Thus began a special friendship that still continues.

Leon turned out to be a gregarious, curly-haired man in his 50s who spoke freely with voice, hands, and heart. Wearing glasses, a plaid shirt, and baggy brown trousers, he met us at the fields on his late-model blue Ford tractor. I have yet to see Leon in jeans or overalls. When we thanked him profusely for his willingness to plow for us, he shrugged and said simply, "If it were to be my daughter needing help, I hope somebody would do it for her." Moreover, he was tickled at the notion of our planting so much ground in gourds.

We were to see evidence many times of Leon Carter's pure, uncomplicated belief in helping his neighbors. His motivation for doing our plowing had nothing to do with the small amount of money he charged for his time.

🦫

Over the years that Leon helped us with plowing and later growing gourds for us on contract, we enjoyed many long, entertaining conversations about gardening and farm life. He often told stories about his muskrat-trapping days or his efforts to rig up his planter to accommodate a special variety of corn or his perennial battle with the beavers in Blue Creek, which bordered his bottom land a little way downstream from the Stovall mill. Though he is of a younger generation than John Head or Ruth Head, Leon is another of the people who gave us treasured glimpses into a way of life already fast-vanishing when we met him.

Janice and I always appreciated Leon's open, friendly way of relating to us. He never asked the dreaded question we heard so often in those days: "Why in the world aren't two nice girls like you married?" He accepted us at face value, became our friend, and put us at ease.

Though he was a part-time Baptist minister and made passing references to his church activities from time to time, Leon never floated questions about our church affiliations, which were non-existent when we first knew him. Both of us found it strange and difficult to be separated from the church, but we were painfully aware of religious teachings against homosexuality, and we were uncomfortable attending church together.

Leon simply said to us, only once, "Hey, if you girls don't have a church home, I'd be proud to have you visit my church." He didn't even wait for an answer, but smoothly made a transition into another subject. We had become accustomed to pointed invitations from well-meaning acquaintances who often invited us to their churches, and therefore we especially appreciated Leon's restraint.

Janice had grown up in the Presbyterian Church and had been active at Clairmont Presbyterian in Atlanta as a young person, teaching Sunday school and singing in two choirs. Her church involvement had been an important focus and a comfort during the time of her parents' divorce when she was 16. Her strong feelings for the church continued into adulthood.

I had come up in the Methodist Church and had also been active as a teenager. Unlike Janice, I had been aware of and fearful about same-gender attractions I experienced as a young person, and I had believed that God would "cure" me if only I prayed hard enough and had strong enough faith. Ironically, the church had been both an agent of my suffering and a comforter as I coped with the terror of my "sickness" by staying very busy with church and school activities.

Both Janice and I had visited churches in our early days of living in White County, but from the time we became a couple in September 1974 we felt we no longer had a place in the church. Although the basic understanding that our love was not morally wrong was crucial to our happiness, we had not focused on theological issues surrounding homosexuality. Neither had we chosen to dwell on feelings of exclusion from church; we'd simply moved on without the church in our lives.

Twelve years of friendship with Leon passed before Janice and I became open about our status as a couple, and even then we never made a point of coming out to him. It seemed unnecessary to force on him a subject we knew he would find unpleasant. Leon Carter would be dismayed and possibly even surprised to learn that his old-maid gourd-girl friends are a same-gender couple, but I don't think he would regret having befriended us.

❧

The Stovall fields, like previous ones, had serious weed problems. But Leon worked the ground repeatedly, first with cutting harrows and then with smoothing harrows, until the soil was fine and loose—a veritable "dust

John Kollock

Janice in her Scarlet O'Hara pose

bed," as he would say. He "laid off" the rows just the right distance apart so that we would be able to plow the spaces between rows with Tiny T.

The day before planting day Janice and I strapped a pillow and a wash-tub to the front of our tractor frame with bungee cords and filled the tub with Rainbow fertilizer. One of us sat on the pillow up front and threw out fertilizer along the row while the other drove, letting the cultivators mix the fertilizer into the soil where the row of plants would be.

We managed to plant all five fields in two days with the help of Mr. Head, who insisted on coming to our aid again that spring. With a hoe in his hand, this gangly man was the picture of grace and economy of motion. He believed in keeping his hoe razor-sharp and was always berating us for using dull hoes: "You couldn't cut through hot butter with them hoes." He would offer to sharpen them for us from time to time, but generally the unspoken rule is that any gardener worth her salt sharpens her own hoe; not to do so would be like fishing with a hook baited by someone else.

While we worked three rows abreast, Janice and I struggling to keep up with him, Mr. Head talked about his childhood. He described his tanned, wrinkled grandmother who had smoked a pipe all her life; his inexplicable childhood habit of stealing hen eggs from the nests in his family's barn and sucking the contents out of them; and his experience as a small boy of being chased by a "hoop snake" that, as his story had it, caught its tail in its mouth and rolled after him for miles before giving up the chase.

Gardening was another subject he never tired of. One of his most-loved mysteries about gardening intrigues me still: "You tell me," he'd say, "how a gourd vine knows if there's a branch of a tree above it to reach for. That vine'll put a runner 18 inches straight up in the air before the runner can grab on a limb, but it knows that limb is there, and it keeps reaching until it can get a grip." There's a sermon in that mystery and in John Head's reverence for it.

After the gourds came up Janice and I gradually learned to use Tiny T to dig out many of the weeds. Making optimum use of the cultivators meant being able to space them on their frames for best effect, and *that* required one of us to learn about such things as wrenches and U bolts. I became the grease monkey in our pair and complained bitterly every step of the way. I had not known a wrench from a pair of pliers up to this point in

John Kollock

Tiny T with Priscilla behind the wheel

my life, and I'd have been happy to keep it that way. Still, the rusty U bolts awaited. We bought a big crescent wrench and a cheap socket wrench set, and somehow I did what I had to, placing the front cultivators so that they would dig about eight inches on each side of the plants and the back ones so that they would dig farther away.

The payoff was thrilling when we began to feel competent at operating our very own tractor. Even now I can think of few experiences to equal that of driving Tiny T over a row of thriving young gourd plants and watching the front cultivators throw just the right amount of dirt to each side of the plants, covering tiny weed sprouts and keeping the soil loose so the roots could grow.

Once one of our cultivators broke off its shaft when it encountered a large rock, and a friend of Mr. Head's came to our rescue. This part-time Baptist minister and part-time welder gently informed us that he didn't approve of two single women trying to be farmers, but he did the job with kindness and courtesy.

It wasn't long before we had minor engine problems, and as a result we met Fred Dean from the Leaf Community, a few miles down the road from Blue Creek. Mr. Dean, a retired mechanic, was a short, stocky man who wore a baseball cap at all times. He was always smiling and always willing to get us going again in a hurry. He developed an affection for Tiny T and called it "the old gentleman." Never wanting to charge us much for his services, only when hard-pressed would he finally say, "Oh, gimme five dollars!"

Farming in general and learning to use Tiny T in particular gave us tremendous respect and admiration for self-sufficient farmers, who must have the skills of a mechanic, welder, meteorologist, and botanist, just to name a few. As for us, we relied on the kindness of competent and sweet-spirited strangers such as Mr. Dean who became our friends.

🐾

Thanks to Leon's initial preparation of the soil and to Tiny T, our third growing season turned out to be just a little easier and more successful than the previous two. The hoeing and sling-blading marathons of the previous years were repeated, but Janice and I took pleasure in working on the Stovall farm. We bought old-fashioned gingham sunbonnets at a craft fair—the kind with a flap in the back to keep the wearer's neck from getting red—and looked like hybrids of liberated women and old-fashioned farm wives in our cut-off overalls, boots, and bonnets. From the middle of April until laying-by time in the middle of July we worked in the fields in the mornings, came home at lunchtime, and made gourd-crafts in the afternoons. Most evenings we returned to the fields and hoed until the lightning bugs came out and we couldn't see well enough to tell the gourd plants from the numerous cockleburs.

When Janice's mother and later my parents came for visits during our first summer at the Stovall farm, we excitedly took them over to show them the fields. At one point during her tour Mama wailed, "I can't believe we sent our baby daughter to college to be a gourd farmer!" She was laughing, but it was true. Her artistic, adventurous self was excited for us and possibly even a little envious, but her protective mother self was fearful about my future. And the part of her that wanted social acceptability for me was completely nonplused at my strange career choice as well as the fact that I had no boyfriends in sight. I was painfully aware of her concerns.

I'm sure there were times when we, too, questioned the wisdom of what we were doing for a living. But mostly we were just happily engaged in the tasks at hand. We had the pleasure of making our first real home together as well as the privilege of working for ourselves. We dreamed of having our own farm, of bounteous gourd crops, and of prosperous weekends at craft fairs. It was enough.

gourd girls

John Kollock

World View

Sometime in early 1979 Janice and I learned about Marvin Johnson, a gourd collector from the Raleigh, North Carolina, area who had grown some round gourds with seed he had obtained from Nigeria. It was time to make our gourd globe.

On an impulse one winter day when we weren't getting along with each other and needed a change of scenery, Janice and I took off on the 300-mile pilgrimage to Mr. Johnson's farm. His ranch-style old-brick home was nestled in a grove of loblolly pines that stretched as far as the eye could see. Mr. Johnson was a tall, round, laughing man with a loud voice who owned thousands of acres of tobacco land in the eastern part of the state. He was friendly enough but obviously enjoyed his role of gourd baron to ours of meek-girl supplicants as I described our dream of making a globe.

We asked that he sell us just one round gourd for any price, but he refused, citing as a reason his protectiveness of the strain of seed he had imported. Janice explained that we wouldn't be cutting the gourd or removing the seed. I even offered to carve him a globe for his own collection in exchange for the gourd, but he did not relent. Though we were disappointed and angry, we didn't betray our feelings but left on friendly terms. After all, he was our only hope.

John Kollock

The gourd earth

Not long after we returned home, a round gourd about ten inches in diameter came in the mail with a note from Mr. Johnson. He promised to send us another as soon as he received his globe. Janice immediately cleaned, dyed, and varnished the gourd. I then spent days carving it, grinding away the ocean and leaving parts of the outer shell to represent the continents and islands. "I don't completely understand the fascination this has for me but know it will lead somewhere," I wrote in my journal. It was hard to let the globe go, but we sent it off to North Carolina as promised. True to his word, Mr. Johnson supplied the second gourd right away, and we made a duplicate globe for ourselves.

The gourd earth was the first in a long line of projects that didn't pay. We took it on the road to craft shows and displayed it proudly—marked "Not for sale." We continued to exhibit mostly in shows in the southeastern United States, although in September 1979 we did travel to a quaint festival in Mount Pleasant, Iowa, called the Midwest Old Settlers and Threshers' Reunion. That fall people there and at shows in Atlanta, Gatlinburg, Tallahassee, Memphis, and Greenville loved the globe, loved seeing the beauty of our planet without countries or borders. They were and still are drawn to the globe in a curious way.

Sales were good that fall, and it is evident from a journal entry that I thought we were leading a charmed life:

> So far things have worked out beautifully for the business;
> one piece after another falls right into place. My feelings
> about this seem to be superstitious—I think of us at times as
> riding on a very fragile streak of luck. . . . I know in my mind
> that this isn't the case—our success is the result of our good
> ideas, hard work, persistence, and positive thinking.

Maybe we *were* successful because we believed we were. However, in financial terms *success* still meant only paying the bills—and our overhead was very low. I don't recall ever thinking about savings, retirement funds, or the fact that we wouldn't stay young forever.

❦

Our third crop, while still far from impressive, was large enough to justify another gourd gathering party. Because fall was our busiest season for craft shows—and because the gourds needed time to begin drying in the fields before being harvested—we established the third Saturday in January as the standing date for the work party. Although winter weather in north Georgia is rarely pleasant for working outdoors, the unlikely timing for our event contributed to its offbeat appeal.

In the early years Janice and I weren't worried about the number of harvesters getting out of hand; we simply opened the party to anyone who wanted to come. The result in1980 was a diverse group of 50 people of all ages from all walks of life. Five or six of them eagerly volunteered their pickup trucks as well.

The task of harvesting was pretty simple: a group of 10 to 12 people went to each of the four fields and fanned out to gather and pile up the gourds, most of which were no longer connected to the dead vines. The only skill required was that of distinguishing the good gourds from the immature ones, which were thin-shelled and sometimes shriveled or cracked. There were always hundreds that had formed too late in the season to mature, and we asked that harvesters stomp the bad gourds they found so that other people could tell at a glance not to bother with them. Gourd-stomping was fun and satisfying, a unique and harmless method of releasing tension. After piles of keepers began to form, the truckers drove around to the mounds, helped load the gourds, and made trips back and forth to unload at our shed behind the house.

Unable to take on the task of feeding 50 people, this time we started the event after lunch and hosted a potluck supper in our house afterward. Harvesters gladly contributed some of their best and heartiest dishes, and the party was a roaring success. People trying to enjoy their overflowing plates of food literally packed our hallway, bedrooms, kitchen, and workshop as well as the living and dining rooms. It was clear that the 900-square-foot farmhouse was too small for such a gathering, but party-goers didn't seem to mind. They couldn't wait to tell their friends what they'd done over the weekend and show off the dated rolling gourd toys they'd received as favors.

We all marveled at the unique sense of community we were creating together, a feeling born of the shared accomplishment of a task and enriched by the humor that always goes hand in hand with gourds.

Although the rolling gourd toys were fun and added variety to our displays at craft fairs, the items that we sold most often were containers, match holders, and Christmas ornaments. The artwork was carved only on the front of these production items, but I made time to carve a few special pieces with all-around wildflower designs. The most ambitious of these, a large gourd container with Queen Anne's lace and lespedeza, took many hours to carve and was perhaps the first creation that made me feel like an artist.

Janice insisted that we put a high price on this piece, and I fully expected that it would never sell. Then Elizabeth and Hal Rhodes walked into our lives in 1981 and bought the gourd as a gift for the newly established Georgia Mountains Museum in Gainesville, where they lived. They made

John Kollock

Queen Anne's lace gourd

the gift in memory of their son, Hal B. Rhodes III, who had been tragically killed the year before. This purchase, which represented a milestone in my artistic life and was part of their healing process, created a special bond. Hal and Elizabeth participated in our gourd gathering parties from that time on and have continued to share in and support the gourd life.

I began to push myself to explore entirely new concepts as well. One that particularly intrigued me was the use of geometric patterns found in nature, e.g., in the center of a horizontal slice of squash. Though most of the designs I carved came from my imagination rather than from actual patterns in nature, they were symbolic of the hidden beauty in nature and of patterns one might see under a microscope. These kaleidoscope designs, as we called them, represented my earliest effort in a continuing search for the secret, magic places where science and art come together.

My fascination with kaleidoscope designs coincided with the decision Janice and I made to create a holiday tree as a donation to the Egleston Hospital Festival of Trees, which was an annual fund-raising event for this children's hospital connected with Emory University in Atlanta. We were way out of our league. The other donors were mostly big-name decorators, but event organizers accepted our offer to donate a gourd tree. I carved 100 one-of-a-kind kaleidoscope ornaments, and together Janice and I designed the setting in which the tree was displayed. All of the trees

Kaleidoscope
designs

Emory Jones

were up for silent auction throughout the week of the festival.

Our gourd tree was the recipient of the highest bid in the festival, thanks to Mildred. Unbeknownst to anyone but Janice and me, she went several times during the event and stepped up the bidding on our entry. The final high bidder at $600, she had the tree delivered to her parents' home, where they enjoyed it for the holidays. Then, by pre-arrangement with us, she returned the ornaments to us and we eventually sold them for $10 each, repaying her for her donation. Everybody won.

That tree—and Mildred's generous-spirited contribution to the effort—were the highlight of the 10 years we participated in the festival, though each year we enjoyed coming up with a different theme for the tree. One year the ornaments were replicas of early American gourd utensils; one year they were pierced ornaments that fitted over the lights on the tree; another year the tree was covered with tiny toy mice, rabbits, elephants, snails, and turtles. The most unusual tree was a sculptural creation built with gourds of all shapes and sizes. Some years we created scenes instead of trees: Gourda Claus with his gourdhead reindeer; Twelve Gourds A-Leaping; and a threesome of gourdhead children caroling. The creative stimulus of the festival was important to me as an artist and later carried over into holiday celebrations after we opened a retail shop.

While the festival was a special time for Janice and me throughout the 1980s, Christmas itself was painful because we were separated, each going to be with her own family for several days around the holiday. On December 25, 1981, I wrote in my journal:

> I'm sorry to admit that for me this season of peace and good will has become more and more one of anger and alienation. I'm angry because I go through this charade every year, hiding my real self. . . . I tell myself I need to somehow "handle" my anger, not let it be destructive for me. But I have to wonder if a stalemate of these proportions isn't more than all the self-help books can teach one to handle.

It would be 10 more years before Janice and I spent Christmas together. We coped with the separation and the anger, somehow managing to enjoy our families in spite of the closet. We understood that they were not to blame for creating the oppressive climate in which we lived.

gourd girls

Gathering Momentum

*O*ur crop in the fall of 1981, the first year we participated in the Festival of Trees, was the best yet. We held the gourd gathering in January of 1982, this time moving the covered-dish supper to the dining hall at nearby Truett-McConnell College in order to accommodate 75 volunteers. The group sang songs after dinner: "Bringing in the Gourds," "I'll Get by With a Little Help From My Friends," and "Wildwood Gourd." Party favors were traditional gourd dippers, each with a hand-printed poem by Po Chii-I attached:

> Men's hearts love gold and jade;
> Men's mouths covet wine and flesh.
> Not so the old man of the stream:
> He drinks from his gourd and asks nothing more.

🌰

In February of 1982 we first exhibited in the Coconut Grove Art Association's annual festival in Miami. It was the first and one of the few truly prestigious shows that saw fit to accept our gourd art, and we were thrilled to have the opportunity to sell there. Moreover, we planned to visit Janice's grandparents in nearby Pompano Beach after the show.

Coconut Grove at that time was an arty and fashionable section of Miami. The show took place in the commercial district amidst galleries, exotic restaurants, and half-dressed pedestrians sporting chains, parrots, or boa constrictors. I don't know how we had the nerve to enter this scene or how we managed to produce all the inventory we took with us. But we hit the jackpot there, selling our humble gourdcrafts as fast as we could bag them between each of the four or five thunderstorms that had us scurrying to cover our tables with plastic. Before we felt it was safe to uncover after each shower, people were already trying to reach under the plastic to make their selections.

We were feeling quite worldly and successful as we headed north toward Pompano Beach after the two-day show ended late Sunday afternoon. Janice's grandparents on her mother's side were Betty and Thomas V. Scott. To Janice, they were Grandma Betty and Grandpa T.V.—pronounced *Grand'ma* and *Grand'pa*, Yankee style. Mrs. Scott was a petite and soft-spoken lady with silver-gray hair and silver-rimmed glasses. Her husband and soul mate, whom she called Scottie, was much taller than she was and very distinguished-looking with his wire-rimmed glasses and silver hair. The couple, both native Pennsylvanians, had retired to south Florida in the 1960s, bought a house in Fort Lauderdale, and eventually simplified by moving into an apartment—an elegant beach high-rise called The Kensington.

The Scotts had been a very important presence in Janice's life, especially during her parents' divorce when she was in her teens. They were reserved and dignified people in their mid-80s who still dined formally each evening, even though at this stage of life their diet consisted largely of Stouffer's frozen dinners. Their furnishings, mostly carry-overs from the 1960s in green, were showing signs of wear, but everything was immaculate and in its place. One of our earliest gourd planters, stuffed with artificial greenery by Mrs. Scott's florist, hung from the arm of a brass floor lamp next to her chair. I had been flattered that she'd liked my work from the beginning despite the fact that gourds were quite foreign to her.

As a first-time visitor in their home, I felt warmly welcomed but aware that a certain decorum must be carefully observed. Janice and I stayed two or three days and enjoyed time on the beach but were reminded regularly by her grandparents to use the service elevator when we were dressed in bathing suits. One evening the Scotts gave a cocktail party for us and invited a dozen of their retired friends. They served "highballs" in glasses that are today in our kitchen cabinets looking wonderfully retro. No doubt the Scotts' friends found us and our stories about the gourd business quite unusual.

We were to be accepted into the Coconut Grove festival twice more before our luck ran out. Each time we did well and enjoyed visiting the Scotts afterward. I was thankful to have a chance to get to know Janice's special mentors while they were still in good form.

Janice and I had a good life, but it revolved around our business and little else. We had many casual friends who liked to come to our gourd parties, but few close friends. People we knew in our age group tended to be earth mother and father types whose lives were focused on their marriages and children; we didn't fit in very well. Though we were invited to some of their social gatherings, we carried our heavy and ill-fitting closet everywhere we went, and our discomfort surely made those around us uncomfortable as well. Even Mildred, our closest friend, was still in the dark about our lifetime commitment to one another.

Experiencing the closet as more and more stifling, I began to lobby Janice for permission to tell a few people about our relationship. She saw the desperation I was feeling but was simply not ready to come out. We both recognized the irony in the fact that the closet itself was bringing about the only serious disagreements between us, conflicts strong enough to threaten our relationship. Both because of and in spite of that fact we began, only just began, to understand the necessity of seeking personal justice in the future.

Sometime in early 1982 Janice did agree that we could tell Mildred, who welcomed our revelation with open arms and was surprisingly comfortable with the dam-burst of talk that came out of us after we felt her acceptance. That crack in the closet door allowed in enough light and air to sustain me until Janice was ready to open it further.

As it happened, we soon formed our first friendship with another lesbian couple, though neither pair came out to the other for several months. We met the two Atlanta women through a mutual friend and began spending quite a bit of time together. But it was not until they invited us to go to the beach that we—with great awkwardness—told each other the whole truth about ourselves. The result was a bond that was life-giving for all of us. After returning from the beach I wrote the following in my journal:

This past weekend Janice and I spent with D and J at the beach. . . . We all felt normal. We shared a lot of ourselves. It's interesting to me to think of how we were on one hand like adolescents—shyly holding hands in each other's presence—and on the other hand very adult, talking coolly about one of the most beautiful and hurtful experiences a person can have.

Around that same time we formed another special friendship when Charlie (Charleen) and Rob Smith came to White County. We had met the Smiths, who'd already been contemplating a move to northeast Georgia, at a craft fair near Calloway Gardens where both of them had worked. They were horticulturists by profession and had begun making containers from various natural materials, including gourds, poplar bark, and wisteria vines.

Rob, who was tall, lanky, and handsome, looked every bit the naturalist in his khaki clothes and safari hat. Charlie was dark-haired, pretty, and had a musical laugh. Although Janice and I were taken aback at seeing for the first time other artists working with gourds, we liked them instantly and found many common interests, including wildflowers. As it turned out, gourds never became their primary craft material; therefore we were spared the angst of being competitors.

When Charlie and Rob gave up their "real jobs" and relocated to our area in early 1981, we showed them around and put them up for a few nights while they looked for a place to live.

Side by side

Janice modeling an avant-gourde mask

The two of them fell in love with the old log cabin on the Stovall farm and began renting it from Ruth Head. They too needed farmland to grow broom corn, strawflowers, and a few gourds, so when spring came along we let them use the field behind the cabin. They were much better farmers than we were, and that field had been our least productive. The four of us became close friends, sharing a special camaraderie born of sitting in the shade together while we took breaks from hoeing and talking endlessly about farming, developing our craft forms, and trying to get accepted into the best fairs.

Janice and I eventually came out to the Smiths, who not only accepted us but asked us to be godmothers to their daughter, Lona Rose, who was born on gourd gathering day in 1982. By harvest time in 1983 she could say "gourd," one of her very first words.

❧

Two hundred years ago when Europeans settled what is now the southeastern United States, they learned about gourds from Native Americans who used them for many purposes, including kitchen utensils, ceremonial rattles, and birdhouses to attract insect-eating purple martins. Settlers incorporated the woody fruits into their own gardens and lives, and eventually the term "gourdhead" came into being as a humorous way to describe anyone who seemed empty-headed. Most people in the South have heard the expression.

John Kollock

A cameraman films "Little Gourd Faunleroy," who was really neighbor Andy Brown

One of the endearing qualities I see in many Southerners is their eagerness to find something funny, no matter how trite and overused, to share as a way of connecting with strangers. Naturally when Janice and I took our crafts to fairs around the South, we were regularly called gourd-heads or told we must be "out of our gourd." Regular exposure to this kind of humor is undoubtedly the reason that the idea of making actual gourdheads came to me. It was an idea so simple and natural that, once conceived, it seemed obvious, and yet I had never seen or heard of it before 1982 when I began making the masks. I cut a hole on one side of a large gourd so that, turned sideways with the stem end as a nose, the whole mask would fit over a person's head. I then cut eyeholes, trying to place them so that the wearer would have some vision. These silly-look-ing heads became a kind of personification of the gourd life.

Although the gourds themselves had plenty of personality and needed no embellishment, I made a series of decorated masks we called the *avant-gourde* series just for the artistic challenge. I placed antlers on one of these to make it look like a moosehead and subsequently began making deer and moose "wall trophies," which gave many laughs to customers and friends—especially folks who didn't like seeing real animal heads displayed as trophies. One woman tried to commission me to make a horse's rear end as a trophy for her to give her ex-husband. I didn't accept the job, but she found a gourd that looked perfect to her and made it herself.

The winter of 1983 once again found a good crop in the Stovall fields. This time the gourd theme party was born when we dubbed the annual gathering, which happened to take place on Super Bowl weekend, the Gourd Bowl. The invitations were Gourd Bowl tickets with an accompanying letter that read in part:

> Dear Friends,
>   Are you tired of sitting in front of your television set watching football games? Or, worse yet, are you fed up with watching others watch bowl after bowl? Well, we here at GOURD TIME PROMOTIONS have just the activity for you—the GOURD BOWL! You need not be a spectator any longer; at the Gourd Bowl you can be a participant! Just imagine yourself passing, punting, and kicking those gourds to safety! Whether you choose to be a player, cheerleader, water person, ambulance driver, or scorekeeper, you'll be an important participant....

Attendance for the Gourd Bowl was at a new all-time high of 100, and the event was covered by an Atlanta TV station. The feature that was aired included shots of "visiting dignitaries," characters such as Little Gourd Fauntleroy and Gourdilocks, played by individuals at the gathering who modeled our new masks for the camera. The covered-dish dinner now moved to the Cleveland Elementary School cafeteria. Favors decorating the tables and given guests as souvenirs were pear-sized gourd cheerleaders waving tiny pennants. The participants themselves were the real cheerleaders who kept Janice and me engaged in the game, happily making it up as we went along.

gourd girls

John Kollock

Blossoming

Our longtime friends John and Nancy Kollock from nearby Habersham County had been among the charter gourd gatherers; I don't think they ever missed a harvest. John, a well-known artist, writer, and historian, was still working a couple of days a week as a commercial artist in Atlanta in the early 1980s and often stopped by to see us on his way home from the city 75 miles southwest of us. In his 50s at that time, John impressed me as exceptionally courteous and refined but quick to laugh. He was an old-fashioned-looking guy with glasses, wavy graying hair, and a Vandyke beard. The three of us took long walks in the pasture while John photographed scenes he wanted to paint and described artistic possibilities he saw. Those times gave Janice and me a treasured view of our beloved corner of the world through the eyes of an artist.

Janice and I often talked with John about our gourd business, and he gave us much encouragement and advice—some of which we actually took. John's unique wisdom and energy are well expressed in words he once said to us that I have tried to remember: "There are two kinds of people in the world—those who do things, and those who sit on the sidelines and criticize." And he added, helping to make it so by his belief in us, "*We* are do-ers."

In the winter of 1983, Janice and I began to wish for a retail shop and gourd museum. Though craft shows as a means of marketing did offer many advantages such as the lack of overhead and the opportunity to travel, we wanted a more permanent venue. On one of John's visits we told him our shop fantasy, bemoaning the fact that we didn't own property and weren't in any position to buy or rent another place. John, ever the advocate for anyone who wants to work hard and make things happen, can always figure out a way.

"Why not build a little building over there to the left of this house?" he asked. "I'll bet Mr. and Mrs. Campbell would let you do that. You're always talking about what nice landlords they are."

The three of us began to get excited about the idea. We reasoned that, if the Campbells were agreeable, we could construct a building that would be movable when the time came to relocate it on our own land. John always has good ideas on demand, rarely needing time for germination. "I think it should have a dogtrot like some 19th-century houses used to have separating the kitchen from the main house. The shop could be on one side and the museum on the other." He grabbed the closest piece of paper, and his right hand began to fly. The sketch that appeared like magic became the shop of our dreams.

With time for reflection, the only point on which we disagreed with John was the size of the building. He worried about our going too far in debt and urged us to keep the building small—around 12' x 30'. But we asserted our independence and decided the shop would be 16 feet wide, the maximum width that would allow an easy future move down the road, and 60 feet long.

Janice and I got busy talking to the Campbells, the bank, and our carpenter friend Roger Brown. By April the building was under construction. It was an exciting time, though the financial commitment was scary. The building would cost about $10,000, and we would take on a payment of $150 per month for 10 years.

Roger Brown, who was smart and resourceful but also laid-back, was the perfect person to be our builder. A beautiful dark-complexioned man around our age with a beard, long hair, and a piercing gaze, he always reminded me of the pictures of Jesus in my childhood Bible. Roger and his two helpers were sweet-natured men whose only vice seemed to be their habit of wandering off the job to go fishing in our neighbors' pond. Even so, they managed to finish the solid pine building almost on schedule and to imbue it with a special ambiance.

We spent every spare moment hanging around our new building while it was under construction. The smell of new wood and the spaciousness of the open-ceilinged, 16' x 36' main display room spoke to us of expanding possibilities. Yet this airy space where we would display the fruits of our labors was in sharp contrast to the closet where our spirits were partially confined. The commitment that was our foundation for the *life* we were building remained not only a secret, but a reason for feelings of alienation from other people. In a journal entry that spring I mentioned in passing my excitement about the new shop, but I gave more space, as most journal keepers are apt to do, to unloading my darker thoughts. After two friends got married on back-to-back weekends that spring I wrote:

> Last Saturday J. and I went to _____'s wedding and this
> Saturday to _____'s. I couldn't help thinking about what our
> own wedding would be like if only we could have one and
> what a joy it would be. . . what a joy it would be if all our
> friends would come and be happy for us. I felt angry and
> resentful when we had to stand with the unmarried girls and
> "try to" catch the bouquets.

Our work had been accepted into a couple of prestigious art festivals for that same spring when the building was going up—one in Oklahoma City in April and one in Beaumont, Texas, in May. We were still driving the 1970 Volkswagen van, and on the way to Oklahoma City it failed us for the first time. In fact, we didn't even make it out of Georgia but had the van towed home from Cartersville and rented a huge Ryder truck, the only one available, for the trip. Janice thought we should take the van trouble as an omen and bail out of the show, but I couldn't give it up. She sympathized with my position and indulged me.

Stressed though we were, we pushed on to Oklahoma City. Our gourds and display pieces filled about 2 percent of the space in the truck, which got about six miles to a gallon of gas; we could almost see the gas gauge moving as we drove. Finally we arrived late on a Friday afternoon in gale-force winds for the outdoor show that was to begin the next day. In continuing high winds we chased gourds all weekend as they flew off our shelves. We barely made expenses and felt lucky to do so. Janice's instincts had been right.

When I think now of our days of traveling to shows and of how young and clueless we were, I know that we were very blessed indeed that the Oklahoma City fiasco was our worst experience. Still, the event did seem to affirm the wisdom of opening a shop.

❧

Because our energies that spring of 1983 were focused on shows and the shop, we decided not to plant a crop at the Stovall farm. Instead we planted about half an acre in front of our new building with the idea that visitors to the shop later that summer would enjoy seeing gourds growing.

By July the building was finished, and we began the work of furnishing our new space. We made plans to host a grand opening celebration on the first Saturday in August and sent out invitations. The open house would take place all day, but there would be special evening hours during which folks could come and see the night blooming of the gourd vines. An unusual characteristic of the species *lagenaria siceraria* is that the blooms open at night and are pollinated by moths and other nocturnal insects. Our vines had covered the rich, newly broken ground in front of the shop and were beginning to bloom profusely by mid-July.

The all-important day finally came, and Janice and I were tired and stressed but excited. Two friends of ours who clowned as a hobby came in costume to help us, but no one else showed up that morning. "They'll be here this afternoon," we reasoned. The day wore on, and the clowns' faces grew sad as only a trickle of people came. Janice and I became more and more embarrassed and heartbroken as the hours passed, but we had to appear smiling and friendly to those few who did come. By the time five o'clock arrived, our spirits were low. We wondered how we could have been foolish enough to think people would actually come to a gourd shop in the middle of nowhere. We were still hopeful that some people would come that evening, but we didn't expect much after the long, disappointing day.

This was not to be the last time we would suffer that kind of angst— not by a long shot. But on that magic summer night in 1983 our spirits were ignited by the bright white gourd blooms and the smiling people they drew to us. At 6:00 the cars began to roll in, and they continued to come for the next two hours. People crowded the little path from the driveway to the new building, which was lighted with gourd candle-lanterns.

John Kollock

Our brand-new gourd shop

Everyone loved the design and contents of the shop; the experience of being served punch on the dogtrot from a gourd punch bowl and dipper; the fun of trying on gourdhead masks. In short, they were delighted to be taking part in the gourd life. Today I have not the slightest idea how much money we made that night—probably not very much. But the payment we received in smiles and inspiration is with us still. A color photograph of Janice and me grinning in the blooming gourd patch, taken by John Kollock, appeared in the Gainesville *Times* the following evening.

❧

Our museum was a special source of delight and interest that night as well. Both Janice and I had always imagined a gourd museum as part of our retail store and for years had been saving examples of many different kinds and shapes of gourds. We'd also made arrangements to lease about 50 museum pieces from American Gourd Society acquaintances who had collected decorated gourds in Nigeria, Peru, and the Orient.

Twenty-two years later our museum boasts a much larger collection of gourds from around the world, all of which belong to us. The presence of these beautiful art objects in our lives has slowly given me a feeling of reverence for them and of connectedness to the people who grew, cut, and decorated the objects. I feel a special kinship with artists whose worlds are very foreign to me but whose livelihoods are similar to my own.

The museum objects have also made me aware of a simple but fascinating connection among the peoples of the earth. As I sit writing at my computer, there is a woman somewhere in northwestern Nigeria engraving designs on a very large gourd bowl that she'll carry on her head to market with grain or milk to sell. In Japan tourists are visiting a shrine at a waterfall where, as legend has it, water was changed to saki inside a gourd. In the little town of Cochas Chicas, Peru, high in the Andes, someone with the last name of Medina, Osores, or Ventura is turning a small flat gourd into a work of art just the way his ancestors have done for hundreds of generations. Somewhere in central Africa a long narrow gourd is being scorched on the inside to make it suitable as a container for milk and cow's blood, a mixture the Masai people give much credit to for their good health. And on the northern coast of New Zealand a fisherman is fastening a gourd float to his fishing line.

Of course we don't need gourds to feel connected to the people of the world; it's our common dependence on the earth to fill our needs, both practical and artistic, that ties us together. Still, I like to think of the gourd life as a metaphor for a life of peaceful and creative pursuits, a life lived in love and respect for all people.

The month of our grand opening, our friend C. P. "Scoop" Scruggs, a retired journalist and lover of novel ideas, took a photo of Janice and me standing in the pasture near our house wearing gourdhead masks. He submitted it to *USA Today*, and it was picked up by *Stars and Stripes* and the Associated Press. The picture appeared in newspapers all over the country—but did not benefit our business. The accompanying clever captions named us as individuals but didn't even allude to the shop. We were disappointed, but Janice did enjoy receiving letters from Lymburners all over the United States.

During the next couple of years articles about our business appeared in *The Atlanta Journal and Constitution* and numerous other publications. A common theme of these articles was often named in the titles: *Thriving Cleveland Industry Makes Art from Gourds; Lowly Gourd Becomes Art Form: Business Is Growing for Two Former Teachers; Out of Their Gourds Springs a New, Lucrative Lifestyle.* What captured the imaginations of journalists was not only the unusual nature of our business and the fact that we had left teaching careers to pursue a different dream, but also the idea that we were growing by leaps and bounds; that our products were in great demand; that we were on the brink of financial success. The articles

John Kollock

Blooming gourd vines on the night of our grand opening

reflected a collective American fascination with the stereotypical "rags to riches" story, the beloved tale of small-town entrepreneurs who make it big.

Janice and I, grateful for the publicity, obligingly took up the age-old script and recited our assigned parts as we had learned them from the culture. Though we never made false claims about financial success, we did fail to recognize and question the assumptions that the American dream was in large part about money and that our own ship was about to come in.

It was true that we were doing well at craft shows and that dozens of stores had approached us about buying our products. We kept a thick stack of business cards from shop owners who wanted to be contacted if we decided to sell wholesale. But our crafts were very labor-intensive to produce, and we had no plans to turn our tiny cottage industry into the manufacturing operation that would have been necessary for us to make much more than a subsistence living.

Janice would have liked to explore the possibility of expanding, but I insisted that life was too short to spend it managing a gourd factory. Moreover, we were both fearful of the health hazards we might create by exposing employees to large amounts of gourd dust and vapors from dye and varnish; as long as we stayed small, our exposure and that of anyone who helped us was limited and manageable. So the gourd factory never

Janice and Priscilla show off museum gourds

happened, and our ship—at least the one full of money—never came in.

We couldn't have articulated the truly significant stories: We were a lesbian couple who had freed ourselves from our fearful dependence on conventional jobs and found a fulfilling way to make a living in our chosen corner of the world. And we had managed to form some special friendships that bridged differences in culture and religion as well as the social handicap of the closet.

❧

The fall of 1983 kept us busy with shows and the shop. Our friend Carey Kollock, John and Nancy's oldest daughter, had come to work for us as a part-time helper before we built the shop and now competently staffed it on weekends when we attended craft shows. A cute, petite young woman with lots of curly brown hair, Carey was in her early 20s and unsure of her career path when she began working with us; she saw the job as fairly short-term, but she liked being able to use her artistic talents and enjoyed the whimsy of it all.

The shop inspired new ideas, perspectives, and marketing possibilities. We now had space enough to offer plain gourds for sale to "do-it-your-selfers," as we called them. Although we'd admittedly felt threatened when we'd begun to see a few other artists beginning to work with gourds, we had the good sense to realize that most of our buyers would not be competitors but just folks who wanted to make a few simple projects for fun. The market for raw gourds has steadily grown for 20 years now and may well be the reason we are still in business. We now have a room—called "Gourd Intentions"—where people can find raw materials, books and supplies. We take pleasure in having introduced hundreds of people to a hobby they have enjoyed, and we frequently receive appreciative comments from them.

Another new effort inspired by the shop was the development of a line of natural gourd utensils. When I had first begun working with gourds, I'd been a purist about wanting to make only items that were my own original ideas; therefore simple traditional items such as bowls and dippers had been out-of-bounds. But somehow the new building, perhaps because of its early American style, inspired me to let go of that self-imposed constraint. I saw that making gourd utensils, which had been around throughout human history, was not at all the same as copying another artist's idea—something I will never do. Gradually we began making colanders, funnels, salt keepers, and garlic keepers as well as bowls and dippers. Now on display in our Gourd-met (as in gourmet) Kitchen, these are still among my favorite items to make because of the history behind them and because I love the idea of people using gourds in their daily lives.

In general Janice, Carey, and I all began to understand and enjoy the benefits of 1,000 square feet of display space as opposed to the 100 square feet we were allotted in a typical craft show. Janice, who took on the role of display designer as well as shop manager, had found her artistic medium. She has an exceptional talent for creating beautiful displays of our work. She also has a way of making visitors feel welcome without intruding on them.

I created a large gourd cash register for our use at the checkout table, making drawers that slid on dowels inside the gourd. The inside parts of the drawers were made of wood, but their fronts were the cutout pieces of gourd that fit back into place. One of the drawers was large enough to hold change and bills, but the smaller ones were mostly for effect. It was a silly idea, and I took a lot of ribbing for it at the time; but it has made people laugh for more than 20 years. I love seeing the occasional sour-faced person break into a grin upon seeing one of us pull out the cash drawer.

We also began creating life-sized gourdhead characters and placing them in the yard for the entertainment of passers-by. The inspiration for the first one came when we were raking leaves the first fall the shop was open and decided to make a gourdhead leaf-raker. We posed him flopped in a pile of leaves right under our sign, mopping his brow. Soon to follow at Thanksgiving was a whole family of gourdhead pilgrims at a picnic table and then Gourda Claus sitting on the dogtrot between the shop and museum. Dozens of other gourdhead characters were to emerge in the years to come.

Though far from drawing large crowds, the shop gradually began to hold its own and sometimes even filled the tiny parking area, which had room for only three or four cars.

A mission began to take shape: encouraging people to be open to nature's inspiration, to the wisdom of foolishness, to unseen possibilities, and to their own creativity. I wrote the following in my journal, sounding a bit self-satisfied but unaware that anyone would read my words:

> Some of the things I originally hoped for—in the beginning when I couldn't accept the fact that I wasn't in a helping profession any longer—are actually true. I believe that seeing our ideas and products excites people in a special way. They really are reawakened to the wonders of nature . . . and want to do more creative thinking of their own.

gourd girls

John Kollock

Gourd Medals

*A*s 1984 approached we decided to stage the Gourd-o-lympic Games in lieu of a harvest. Since we'd planted only the half-acre patch in front of the shop the previous spring, our crop was very small. The gathering wouldn't take more than 15 minutes. So we sent out letters and registration forms, complete with a Gourd-o-lympic logo—five interlocking gourds configured like the circles in the official logo—and planned events such as the gourdiscus throw, stomp-the-gourd competition, and gourd sandwich race. Willingness to play the fool was the only qualification necessary to enter our Games.

We wanted to open the ceremonies with the lighting of a gourd torch, and Mildred Neville volunteered to do the honors, wearing a gourdhead mask. I made the torch from a large dipper-type gourd, cutting it off at the widest point so that, held upright by the handle, it looked like the real thing. Mildred secured a can of Sterno inside the torch and practiced running with it while wearing the gourdhead. She spent a lot of time figuring out how to stabilize the large gourd on her head so she could run safely for a distance of 200 yards or so. Her hard work paid off.

The day of the Games arrived, a perfect January day in northeast Georgia: the air was very cold, but the sun shone warmly. The borrowed bleachers facing our gourd patch were filled with 100 enthusiastic athletes

Mildred lighting the torch for the 1984 Gourd-o-lympic Games

and spectators aged 1 to 91. The official Olympic theme music began to play, and our torch bearer came into view, running down Blue Creek Road toward the field in front of our shop building. Everyone cheered loudly as Mildred arrived at the playing field and lit the official torch, a stately looking large roundish gourd that, also holding Sterno, was attached to the top of a pole beside the podium. Strange to say, it was a tear-jerker moment. People were cheering, I believe, for the gourd life, the *joie de vivre* we were all at that moment helping to sustain in each other.

Two news crews were on hand to cover the Games, one from WXIA in Atlanta and one from WGTV in Athens. Although the crew members had not intended to participate, they found themselves entering events and attending the dinner that evening. One couple even returned to participate in the gathering the following year.

The potluck awards banquet was again held at the elementary school. Fortunately we had a surplus that year of flat, round ornamental gourds a little larger than a silver dollar, which made perfect medals. We awarded a gold, silver, and bronze medal for each event; spectators and losers received plain gourd medals, so everybody won.

❧

Like Mildred carrying the torch, Janice and I hit our stride that year in many ways—but we also broke our stride as gourd farmers. Having skipped a season of gourd growing and taken on the large commitment of operating the retail shop, we could not envision a return to farming at the Stovall fields.

So in the spring of 1984 we gave up large-scale farming and began putting our energy in other places. Leon Carter, who owned four acres of rich bottomland close by and was ready for a change from growing corn, agreed to grow gourds for us on contract. We would still have our gourd gathering parties to harvest Leon's gourds, and we would continue to tend our patch in front of the retail shop.

I am sad now as I think of the end of our serious farming days and of the changes that were coming at the Stovall place. Ruth Stovall Head was already in a nursing home, and the sale of the precious family property was just around the corner. Today houses and resorts occupy the land where we hoed, sling-bladed, sweated, itched—and, despite it all, gloried in being farmers. The shady little dirt paths we walked to the fields with such anticipation are now wide paved roads leading to the homes of people who were never privileged to hear Mrs. Head's stories of growing up on that land in the early 1900s and loving it as much as life.

❧

Janice and I bought a brand-new Dodge van—dubbed Gourdon—that spring and took it on the road to a profitable show in charming Fairhope, Alabama. The following July we took the van to Martha's Vineyard Island, Massachusetts, the 15th state we had visited with our gourdcrafts. Seeing the show as an opportunity to write off a vacation, we invited my parents to come along for the trip.

Martha's Vineyard is home to several unique communities on different parts of the island. Not knowing what to expect, we had made reservations in the town of Oak Harbor, which turned out to be the loudest and most touristy of all the areas. Our hotel rooms were above a piano bar, and we discovered how hot "up North" can be in July. Though we loved seeing the island, the show itself was not as profitable as we had hoped; the wealthy New Englanders, who taught this Southern girl the meaning of reserve, did not run up to our booth exclaiming over the gourds and buying everything in sight as I had imagined they would do.

For the four of us it was a fun trip together, but as always when we spent extended time with family, Janice and I found it hard to breathe inside our invisible closet. I was always on guard, always fearful that something would happen to give us away. I thought Mama and Daddy must have sensed my discomfort and that it must have been both a mystery and a subtle source of pain for them.

We were a little more comfortable with Janice's mother during our years in the closet than we were with my parents. When we were with Nancy, who had been divorced from Janice's late father for many years, it was just "us girls." Our perception was that Janice's failure to marry didn't worry Nancy as my unmarried state did my parents, whose own experience had taught them that marriage brought happiness. Mama and Daddy were considerate about not bringing up the subjects of dating and marriage after I reached a certain age, but I feared that they were sad about my not having found—to their knowledge—a life partner.

It wasn't long after the Martha's Vineyard trip that my parents and Janice and I decided to buy a seven-acre piece of land near the Campbell farm and divide it between us. Mama and Daddy had fallen in love with our area and dreamed of a second home in the mountains. Although I couldn't admit it to myself at the time, I know now that I was painfully ambivalent about their increasing presence in our lives. I loved them deeply, and in fact as the "baby" in our family I had been a little too attached to my parents as a child; so I was pleased that they shared my love of northeast Georgia and wanted to be near me. Yet the closet took away some of my pleasure in being with them.

The property we bought was perfect in that it was within easy walking distance of our business and offered pretty views of Yonah from at least two different building sites. Janice and I were able to afford our half of the property only because my paternal grandmother, Mary Wilson—known to hundreds of people who loved her as Mae Mae—offered to match whatever funds we could put into the land. Janice drew her teacher retirement money from the state of Georgia, and with the matching gift we had exactly enough for our part of the purchase price.

Beautiful even in old age with her fine features, aristocratic forehead, and an aquiline nose I always envied, Mae Mae was a petite, sparkling Southern lady and one of the great loves of my life. She had a magic way of encouraging Janice and me by her generosity of spirit as well as her financial gifts.

When I first left Mae Mae's own early profession of teaching and started the gourd business, she had difficulty understanding why I would want to do such a thing. To an educated southerner of her generation, gourds must have seemed a strange choice indeed for an artistic medium or a business. In the early days she more than once squinted at me with a puzzled, slightly pained expression, and asked gently, "But dahlin', why go-uhds?"

I'll always believe that it was Janice's entry into the business that turned Mae Mae around and helped her get excited about the "go-uhd" business. She was crazy about Janice and had an instinctive knowledge that we made a good pair, although she likely was unaware of the phenomenon of homosexuality. Much to everyone's surprise and dismay, Mae Mae often commented enthusiastically to friends and relatives in our presence, "Don't you think Priscilla and Janice complement each other?! I just think they are so *good* together!" No one knew how to respond to her outbursts of love for the two of us together; she was dangerously close to violating an unspoken code of language observed by family members of closeted gays and lesbians. I don't know which side of the closet door was more uncomfortable in those moments. But her approval of us and our partnership was life-giving to us, so much were we in need of acceptance from our families.

In the same spirit as she had made look-alike Easter dresses for my sister, cousin, and me when we were children, Mae Mae once bought look-alike blouses for Janice and me to wear at craft fairs. We didn't know whether to laugh or cry; we didn't want to hurt her feelings, but neither could we imagine ourselves dressing alike. I thanked her profusely, made excuses about the blouses not fitting us, and returned them to the store. She must have been puzzled because of my inability to explain to her honestly that, even had we wanted to dress alike, we couldn't have done so because of our fear of looking like a couple.

In the summer of 1984, soon after our property purchase, Janice and I started in motion an effort to form an artists' guild for the purpose of hosting a holiday studio tour and sale. It was an idea that had been tossed around among artist friends for years. Finally, realizing that many good ideas go undone for lack of someone to make the first move, we planned an organizational meeting and invited nine artists we liked and whose work we admired, including Rob and Charlie Smith and John Kollock. The Foothills Guild of Art and Crafts was born and held its inaugural tour on the first weekend of December 1984.

The tour was a great success and continues to be held annually after twenty-two years. Quite a few artists have come and gone over the years, but a few founding members remain, including John Kollock, who designs artful brochures for the group every year. Although the guild exists for the primary purpose of holding the tour, our regular meetings have given us a chance to socialize and share informally in one another's artistic journeys.

gourd girls

Great Gourd Giveaway

Leon Carter grew bumper crops of gourds in his four-acre bottom-land field in 1984 and for several years thereafter. Thus gourd gathering as a serious winter sport came into its own in the mid- and late 1980s, and the evening parties became increasingly elaborate. Inspired by the annual deluge of advertising in January by Publishers' Clearinghouse, Janice, Carey, and I decided to dub our 1985 party the Gourdcrafters' Clearinghouse Great Gourd Giveaway. Carey, though she might have characterized herself as shy, was as much of a theme party enthusiast as we were and was to become a star of sorts that year.

The invitation, tongue-in-cheek as usual, read:

Dear_____,

Have you received so many sweepstakes offers lately that you are confused, anxious, and don't know which one to enter? Well, fret no more! Gourdcrafters' Clearing House has the sweepstakes for you! How would you like to win a new car, house, yacht, or computer? Just imagine yourself as the proud owner of one of these fabulous gifts! And it's so easy! Simply return the attached entry blank and follow a few simple rules to ensure your eligibility.* We at Gourdcrafters'

Clearing House guarantee that you will win a prize!**
Gourdgeous gifts await you! Don't delay!

*To be eligible for prizes in the Great Gourd Giveaway, entrants
must participate in the Great Gourd Gathering from 2:00 to
5:00 p.m. on Saturday, Jan.19, and the covered-dish supper to
follow. Entrant should be aware of certain hazards such as
cockleburs, cold weather, backaches, mud, confusion, and long
bathroom lines.

**Your prize might not be one of those mentioned above.

The number of gourd gatherers grew that year to well over 100 people
who harvested thousands of gourds and seemed to enjoy the task more
than ever. I was the field boss and Janice was the boss of the storage shed.
Over the years she had begun to develop a crew of people who counted
and sorted the gourds like clockwork as the trucks brought load after load
from the field. She took much kidding about what a tough taskmaster she
was, but her ability to organize that end of the operation was crucial. And
those folks who weren't physically able to work in the field had a place at
the shed where they could be of real help.

There were 8 or 10 trucks participating that year, most notably the
Nevilles' old 1950 Chevrolet, by now considered indispensable, and our
landscaper friend Eddie McLean's huge old truck, which everyone called
"Big Red." Big Red was a serious hauler of gourds, the tough jock of the
fleet driven by the ever-cool Eddie as though he trucked gourds every day.

The after-dinner program at the elementary school was a quiz show
that was a cross between "Let's Make a Deal" and "Wheel of Fortune."
Janice played the MC, a Monty Hall character complete with red jacket,
mustache, and slicked-back hair; Carey and I were stage assistants, calling
ourselves the Gourdettes. Our skimpy gourd costumes brought down the
house and were never equaled in future years. We wore leotards under the
gourds but still looked sleazy, at least by gourd-girl standards. I'm embarrassed now when I see our photographs, but we did make gourd history.
In subsequent years, no matter what kind of skits were performed, people
in the audience always yelled, "Bring out the Gourdettes!"

Each attendee was given a gourd key chain favor with a number
attached that was used in selecting contestants for the game. We gave away
a house, car, boat, and computer (an abacus)—all made from gourds.

John Kollock

Janice as MC with "Let's Make a Gourd Deal" contestant Thelma Neville

By the time of the next gathering in 1986 Janice and I had a house under construction. The division of the seven-acre plot had been easy; my parents preferred the wooded portion that was a little higher up and gave a spectacular view of Yonah Mountain, while Janice and I preferred the cleared part of the land, which offered a half-acre gourd-garden spot on one side of our future house.

With the help of our good friend and talented house designer Gloria Brown, we had come up with a plan for a simple and affordable house and contracted with another friend, Jimmy Johnston, to build it. Both Gloria and Jimmy had been gourd gatherers almost from the beginning.

During the house planning process, Gloria became the only person who ever tried to coax us out of the closet. Although we had known and liked Gloria for years, she was not one of the handful of people who knew of our relationship. So in spite of the fact that we were on a tight budget, we had told her each of us would need a bedroom—even though in reality we shared a room like any other couple.

Finally one day, as she struggled with us to find ways to save space, she

John Kollock

Janice as the Fairy Gourdmother

blurted: "For heaven's sake! Why do you need two bedrooms and a guest room? You can save a lot of money by having just one bedroom and a guest room!" She was careful not to be too specific or corner us verbally, but it was clear that she was knocking on the closet door.

We were too shocked to say much of anything that day, but the next day we made our awkward coming-out speech to her, swearing her to secrecy as we did every person to whom we came out for years. What a comfort it was to be able to talk openly with her about our real needs, including the need to make the appearance of two bedrooms so we could shield our families and other guests from the truth. We decided with her help to limit ourselves to two bedrooms and no guest room. When company came, one of us would pretend we didn't mind giving up our room for them and sleeping together. The closet could be complicated and expensive, both literally and figuratively.

❧

It was only a short walk through a neighbor's pasture from the gourd shop to the construction site, so on gourd gathering day everyone walked over and toured our almost-finished house. I remember people grinning and saying in amazement, "It's the house that gourds built!" I hope the veteran gatherers understood that they had helped to build it—not only with their harvesting help, but by pulling for us to succeed with our business.

The party theme that year was *Once upon a Gourd Gathering*. Our invitation had billed the evening program as a production by the "world-renowned Gourd Time Players, starring the One—the Only—Fairy Gourdmother and a cast of thousands." Admission to this production was "three hours hard labor and a covered dish." In the skit I played a proverbial young woman in search of meaning, and Janice played the Fairy Gourdmother, who taught the girl about the need for gourds in her life. As a way of illustrating the importance of gourds, the Gourdmother described little-known roles played by gourds in stories such as *Cinderella, Snow White*, and *Hansel and Gretel*. In this way various audience members were brought into the skit as fairy-tale characters with quirky props or costume parts made from gourds.

Although the production was unapologetically haphazard, the Gourdmother's words to the girl at the end of the story were profound: "Gourds will bring you friends, and friends will bring you gourds." We gave each person a tiny decorated gourd holding "magic seed" to take home as a favor.

gourd girls

John Kollock

The House That Gourds Built

$\mathcal{E}$arly in the spring of 1986 we moved into our new home. The wood siding was stained dark brown on the outside to look like one of the creosoted cabins at Camp Toccoa where Janice and I had met, but on the inside the house was open and full of light, all windows and natural wood and white Sheetrock. The large windows and glass doors on the front gave us wonderful views of our beloved Mount Yonah.

Our bedroom was upstairs, along with my studio space. I remember waking up those first spring mornings with a heightened awareness of airy space, light, possibilities—and of the hauntingly beautiful three-note song of a red-winged blackbird outside the window, a melody that remains a musical theme of my life. I felt wonderfully free of a burden, the burden of proving we could become homeowners and thus make it in the world.

We continued to rent the Campbells' farmhouse as our workshop and to operate our retail shop next door as before. Finally we had more than enough space for producing, storing, and marketing our gourdcrafts. And the move away from our workspace gave us a sense that we could have a life apart from the business. We had been immersed in the task of creating Gourdcraft Originals and had few interests beyond that, but now new energy flowed for both of us. I began taking piano lessons for the first time since junior high school and writing a weekly column for our local newspaper.

Janice enjoyed designing and planting flowerbeds in our very own yard.

We planted gourds as well as garden vegetables in the half-acre patch beside our house and now cultivated it along with the similar-sized patch in front of the retail shop. Keeping up the two gourd gardens with our tractor was a "play job," as Mr. Head would have called it, compared with our earlier farming challenges. John Head had died in 1985 after a brief battle with lung cancer, and Ruth Stovall Head, our other gardening mentor, died soon after. We remained—and still remain—mindful of their influences.

&

Life was good, but too soon everything changed in the fall of 1986, when my mother was tentatively diagnosed with ALS, better known as Lou Gehrig's disease. This is a progressive fatal neuromuscular disease that gradually leaves its victims completely paralyzed. Our family was devastated. I woke up every morning crying. A couple of days after receiving the news I wrote in my journal:

> I think I had secretly wondered if I lacked the ability to care
> as deeply as others, if I was maybe flawed in some way so
> that I couldn't respond as I'd be expected to in a family
> crisis. Well, I've learned about myself in the last two days that
> I'm quite capable of grieving.

Now I understand the entry better than I did at the time I wrote it. Because of the closet, I had distanced myself emotionally from my family and had been feeling deeply angry about their failure to magically know the truth, convey their acceptance, and open the heavy closet door that we weren't strong enough to open for ourselves. I had come to doubt my own love and loyalty, which in reality were very strong.

I found it difficult to work, but Janice and I had shows scheduled and financial commitments. We spent as much time as possible with Mama and Daddy that fall, and all of us took comfort in being together. We talked and cried about ALS but tried to remain hopeful that tests to be repeated in January would prove the diagnosis wrong. Mama used humor as a coping mechanism and often quipped when she teared up, "Oh, don't mind me. I even cry at store openings, you know."

Mama's second test for ALS happened to be administered on the Friday before the 1987 gourd gathering was to take place on Saturday. I

1987 gourd gatherers in front of the Campbell farmhouse

called my parents that night and learned the bad news: her diagnosis was confirmed. Mama managed to sound matter-of-fact on the phone, but I was so grief-stricken that I could scarcely make my voice work. I felt I betrayed her by letting my grief show.

The next day's event was both difficult and comforting for me. It was hard to keep a stiff upper lip, but it was wonderful to be surrounded by friends. Our program for the party that year was an initiation service of a mock fraternity we called Gamma Alpha Gamma Gamma, or Georgia Association of Gourd Gatherers. John Kollock created a cartoon crest for GAGG that featured a bust of our oldest member, Mildred's father, Rae Neville, with his hair matted in cockleburs; an old truck full of gourds; and a booted foot stomping a rotten gourd. The formal invitation to the event, complete with crest, read:

> Dear Prospective Gamma Alpha Gamma Gamma Initiates:
>   We trust that you are as delighted to receive this sacred invitation as we are to extend it to you in this our 10th year. A moving and awe-inspiring ritual of initiation awaits you. Please study your metaphysics, fast for five days, and limber up in preparation for the ceremony.
>
>   Yours in the mystery of the gourd

When the gatherers arrived at the Cleveland Elementary School cafeteria that evening for the covered-dish dinner and program, the long

Elder Nancy Kollock reading a lengthy charge to prospective members during the GAGG initiation ceremony

tables were lined with gourd candle holders for use in the initiation rites and as take-home favors. Six GAGG members who had participated in every gathering were designated elders, given ponderous gourd hats to wear, and seated in places of honor on the stage. After the requisite "mystical" songs and readings had been performed, each of the 125 GAGG members came up on stage in order of seniority and lit a candle to signify their initiation. The youngest initiates were babies in arms, and the oldest were in their 80s and 90s. After the lighting of the candles the secret handshake and password were revealed. The handshake has long been forgotten, but the password stuck: "One gourd turn deserves another."

Mama and Daddy came for a visit right after the gathering. While they were with us we had a big snow, and Janice and I needed to throw out hay for the cattle at the Campbells' place. It was a chore we often performed for them in bad winter weather. Mama wanted to get out in the snow, so all four of us walked over to the barn. It was the kind of stunning morning that happens only when fresh snow, deep blue skies, and sunshine collaborate. All of us were lost in the beauty around us, snow-blinded into a brief state of euphoria and forgetfulness of our grief and fears.

For days afterward I could see all of our tracks in the snow, including those made by Mama's newly acquired walking cane.

gourd girls

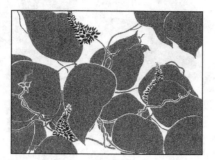

Shades of Green

$\mathcal{M}$y creative energy that year was strong. I believe this was due not only to the fact that our striving for a house was behind us, but also to my mother's illness. ALS is fatal for most victims in three to five years, and I experienced vicariously my mother's heightened gratitude for each day of life. I was aware of a strange paradox in which pain can give rise to joy and therefore new energy.

In February 1987 I began working on an idea Janice and I had been discussing for several months: creating a line of wildflower T-shirts. At that time printed Tees usually bore business names, messages, or cartoon-like graphics; rarely did they display art. Most were printed either in one color or full color, but the two-color, stylized wildflower prints we envisioned would make silk-screened T-shirts something of an art form. Janice saw this as a good business idea in that, once I had created the designs, they could be mass-produced by a screen printer. She wanted me to have some relief from the repetitive artwork I was doing on the gourds; and she somehow knew she would be successful in marketing the shirts to wholesale buyers.

I had a vision of the prints I wanted to create, but I knew nothing of the technical art of putting them on paper for reproduction via the silk-screening process. It was my good fortune that in 1987, when the

John Jones

John Kollock in his studio in the 1980s

world of graphic design was on the brink of change, I had in John Kollock a teacher who knew and loved the old materials and methods. John took me into the cozy, book-lined studio on his family compound in Habersham County and treated me like a real artist. His studio, which smelled like an old-fashioned stationery store, was suffused with a soft, steady, and contagious artistic energy born of years of John's talent being put to good use.

John, who had worked as a commercial artist in Atlanta for many years to earn the means to stay on his ancestral home place and be a full-time watercolorist, knew the language of graphic arts better than any teacher I could have hoped for. He explained the color separation and silk-screening processes to me and showed me how to draw my designs with a crow-quill pen and India ink or paint them with gouache, depending upon the requirements of a particular design.

Soon I had four camera-ready wildflower designs to take to the printer: toadshade trillium, bloodroot, yellow violet, and fire pink. Janice and I took them to a small locally owned printing company called Bluegraphics in nearby Cornelia and placed our first order. We instantly liked the owner, David Overton, with whom we shared baby-boomer status, old-hippie values, and independent spirits.

As soon as the shirts were printed Janice took samples to several shops and galleries in White and Habersham counties to test the waters. She came home beaming, with orders for dozens of shirts. Not long after that we invited Janice's mother, Nancy, to go with us to Calloway Gardens, a large attraction in west-central Georgia, for a wildflower workshop. While we were there we showed our samples to the gift shop manager, who promptly ordered 10 dozen shirts. Suddenly we were in the T-shirt business. We called our new product *BLUE CREEK VALLEY distinctive plant life designs.*

Although I was the wildflower artist, Janice and I were very much a team in choosing design concepts and color combinations. She always tried—with great difficulty—to keep me in tune with the tastes of the buying public. Janice also managed the business end of the new line, from ordering blank shirts to coordinating with Bluegraphics to shipping out wholesale orders.

We spent many hours standing beside David's silk-screen presses while he and his employees patiently mixed shade after shade of green ink until we found the one that suited the plant and looked good on the shirt color we had chosen for a particular design. Mountain laurel foliage required a dark green while pink lady's slipper needed a soft, gray-green, and fire pink a grass green. Almost every plant design required a different shade. I came to like the familiar chemical smell of the ink and of hot T-shirts as they came off the conveyer belt of the special dryer that cured the ink.

I created new designs in bursts of energy, usually spending 10 to 20 hours on each one. My first step, even when I worked with a familiar species, was to spend time sketching the plants in the woods or on the roadside where they were growing. It was important to me that my drawings be of real plants, not just made-up plants with correct botanical features. Renditions of specific plants were like portraits to me, each intended to record a living being's existence at a given moment in time.

Because I lacked training and didn't draw particularly well, I relied on the process of trusting my eyes and faithfully recording exactly what I saw. It was a foolproof method of capturing my subject and thus passing myself off as an artist. Often lying on the ground at eye level with the plants to get the proper perspective, I learned what all representational artists learn: one cannot truly know a subject except by making a detailed drawing of it. My relationship with wildflowers became more intimate than ever.

Carey Kollock, who was still helping us when we first started the T-shirt business, half-jokingly suggested that I use kudzu, a very invasive plant that has become a serious problem in the southeastern United States, for one of the designs. The idea struck a chord with me, and soon the "Unpopular Plant Series" was born. Poison ivy and deadly nightshade, commonly known as horse nettle, eventually became part of the series, but the kudzu design was our all-time best-selling shirt.

Eventually we produced a series of holiday shirts, which included such plants as Christmas fern, wild poinsettia, and star-of-Bethlehem; a Budding Botanist Series for children, which included blue sailors, bouncing Bet, and Johnny jump-up; and even special shirts commissioned by the Harvard University Arboretum and Calloway Gardens. In the five years or so that the T-shirt business boomed, we and Bluegraphics together created T-shirts bearing 35 different plant designs that were sold to about 50 different stores. It was an exciting time for us. Our shirts seemed to be everywhere in our local area, and I'm sure people thought we were making lots of money. The reality was that we had hit on another good idea that didn't pay particularly well; our profit margin was relatively small

Modeling T-shirts for a color brochure: left to right, front row: *Charlie Smith, Margaret Kollock, John Kollock, Priscilla Wilson, Courtney Johnston;* back row: *Carey Kollock, Nancy Kollock, Rob Smith, Jim Johnston, Janice Lymburner*

after we paid for the Tees and the printing. Still, we hoped financial rewards would be just around the corner. We were too busy to think much about profits.

On the day I entered the ninth grade my civics teacher asked each student to write an autobiography in class. When she returned our papers the next day, she offered to "analyze" anyone who wanted to stay after class, basing her conclusions on what we had written. When my turn came, she summed me up in five words: "You are bored with life." I heard those words as a terrible indictment.

As I recall, she responded to my stricken face by explaining that I had written the history of my life in a way that made it sound very humdrum. In my view, I had indeed hurried through the facts of my life but had done so in an effort to get to the interesting part: the present. Still, there must have been some truth in her statement, because it hurt and haunted me into adulthood.

Then came Janice, and then the gourd business, and I was happily conscious of not being bored. Especially during the years of drawing those early wildflower designs, I had a heightened sense of engagement, gratitude, and well-being. One day when I sat down to work at my drawing board, I found a quotation that Janice had copied and placed there for me. It was from Thomas Carlyle: "Blessed is he who has found his work. Let him seek no other blessedness."

Gourd-o-cratic Old Party

*D*uring February 1987, while I was working on the first of the Blue Creek Valley designs, Janice and I had a call from our former summer camp in nearby Toccoa. The oldest cabin in the camp was to be torn down and replaced by a new administration building; the director was offering us the cabin free if we would have it moved.

At the time of Mama's ALS diagnosis, my parents had been making plans to build a house on their property adjacent to ours, but since the diagnosis they had not been able to focus on the project. Janice and I offered them the camp cabin, and they accepted. They would be able to have a small and historic mountain home without the delays, expense, and stress of building. We wasted no time arranging for the site clearing, building move, and foundation construction. By the end of March the cabin was in place about 100 yards behind and above our house, ready to be renovated. By summer Mama and Daddy were spending time there. Mama, who had always needed creative projects to make her happy, found a perfect diversion in making curtains and decorating the cabin. She was still ambulatory, though she was using a walker, and her hands had not yet been affected by her disease.

For the next four years my parents spent a couple of months at the cabin each spring and fall. During that time Mama's condition deteriorated relentlessly, but she took great pleasure in being in their mountain home. She had a perfect view of Mount Yonah from the cabin porch, and it became the comforting friend to her that it had been to us for so long. She delighted in watching infinite shades of green climb up the mountain in the spring and eventually turn to infinite shades of orange, gold, and red that made their way back down our Yonah in the fall. Mama spoke often of her deep feelings for the mountain and mentioned more than once that she might like her ashes to be taken there when she died.

Although visitors to our shop often told us how envious they were of our laid-back lifestyle, the truth was that Janice and I lived frenzied lives in those years. We wanted to spend time with my parents while they were at the cabin and did share most suppers and evenings with them, but we always had an endless amount of work in front of us as well. Like most any daughter of a sick mother, I was plagued by the knowledge that I could never do enough, could never make everything okay for her as she had been able to do for me in my childhood.

The idea of ever telling my mother the truth about my love for Janice had become unthinkable from the moment we learned of her illness. I could not consider adding more pain to her already unbearable load. Thus I felt an unshakeable sadness about the fact that, as deeply as she loved me—and she was motherly love personified—she would never know the most important fact of my life. She would die unaware that I had found the person who loved me and would share the rest of my days.

Family crises always place a strain on primary relationships, and this one was no exception. Janice cared deeply for my parents and they for her, but the fact that they were unaware of her preeminence in my life made it especially difficult for her to give up as much of me as I was asking her to do. I was a bundle of stress as I tried frantically to please everyone and create an *esprit de corps* among the four of us without that essential bonding tool called truth. As I look back now, I know that my desperation must have been as exhausting to everyone in my presence as it was to me.

In spite of it all, the creative spark stayed alive. In 1988, an election year, we dubbed our gourd gathering party the "Gourd-o-cratic Old Party Convention." The invitation featured Uncle Sam as a gourdhead soliciting "delegates":

Harvesters in Leon Carter's field

> Now is the time for all gourd folks to come to the aid of
> their party! The Gourd-o-cratic Old Party National
> Committee has decided to get a jump on all the other par-
> ties by holding our convention early in 1988—January
> 16—at the Gourd Time Convention Center. At this time
> we will nominate our candidate for the presidency and
> kick off our campaign. Join us and make your voice heard!

The "convention schedule" listed a "required recreational activity" of
gathering gourds. Leon Carter had grown a particularly large crop that
year, but harvesting conditions weren't good; the ground was too soft to
drive on. We tried using litters and various other methods for carrying
large numbers of gourds, but everything proved impractical; the reality
was that trucks needed to be driven into the huge field. Most truck owners were willing to give it a try even though they were likely to get stuck.
Time after time, trucks had to be pushed out of the mud. People were
good-natured about this extra hardship, but some of the large men in the
group were undoubtedly very tired and sore that night.

Gourd gatherings were always fraught with problems relating to
weather, mud, and the logistics of organizing 100–150 volunteers to do a

Victorious candidate P. Martin Gourd, played by Dusk Weaver, with a ci-gourd in his mouth; on the left, Tom Landreth and Rosie Clark

John Kollock

large job in a few hours. Janice and I worried obsessively each year about conditions but then had to accept what nature gave us and, harder yet, the generous, judgment-free help of GAGG members. Being the recipients of such help was a heart-opening and humbling experience.

The political convention program was one of my personal favorites. Janice, Carey, and I had invented three candidates in advance, written speeches, and recruited GAGG members to play their parts. Candidates were Mr. P. Martin Gourd, so-named for purple martin birdhouse gourds; Ms. Lagenaria Vines, employing the Latin name for the most common species of gourd; and Col. Beauregourd C. Burr, for the cockleburs with their sandspur-like seed cases that plagued gatherers each year.

Convention attendees were given the requisite Panama hats and encouraged to make signs or otherwise act the parts of enthusiastic delegates. At least one sign purporting to be sponsored by a truck pushers' union appeared during the evening. I delivered the rousing keynote address standing on a large, flat gourd:

> Ladies and gentlemen, I stand before you on a gourd platform as I say to you that all of our nation's problems can be solved with gourd attitudes such as humility, neighborliness, diligence, and a sense of humor. But have the other parties' candidates ever gathered a single gourd? [Nooooo!]
>
> Have they performed the humble task of extricating cockleburs from the heads of their companions? [Nooooo!]
>
> Have they known the sheer existential pleasure of stomping a rotten gourd? [Nooooo!]
>
> The appalling truth, ladies and gentlemen, is that the other parties don't even know that gourds exist! Can you in good conscience allow such a person to be elected President of the United States of America? Of course not! So, on with the task of nominating our candidate!

After the three candidates gave their campaign speeches to the rowdy crowd, the convention elected P. Martin Gourd as the party's nominee. In retrospect I see that the Gourd-o-cratic Old Party did indeed have something special to offer our country.

gourd girls

Jim Reeves

Wildflower Dreams

On our long walks in the pasture during the winter of 1988, Janice and I began dreaming of opening a wildflower shop to showcase our T-shirts and other wildflower-related products. On March 21, the first day of spring that year, we held a successful grand opening of a tiny shop, which we called *Wildflowers.* We had moved our gourd museum into the front of our former house, now the workshop building, so the wildflower shop could be located in the retail building.

In addition to T-shirts, books, seed, and prints, we displayed small wooden stools with native plants beautifully painted by my mother, who took much pleasure in doing something productive to help us with our new endeavor.

Our friend Nancy Kollock gave us the idea of creating an educational display of wildflowers currently in bloom as a feature in the new shop, and people enjoyed this immensely. We picked samples of non-endangered wildflowers on our daily walks, placed the specimens in small glass bottles of water, and labeled each with the name of the flower. Our "Now in Bloom" display, now in its 17th year, continues to delight people and pique their interest in native plants. We're always gratified to see regular visitors make a beeline to the display, often dragging their guests with them. "You've got to see this," they say, or "Hmm . . . butterfly weed—so *that's* the beautiful orange flower I've been seeing on the roadside" or "Gee, I've always loved seeing these bluets, but I never knew their names until now."

Some people don't believe it's necessary to learn the names of wildflowers in order to enjoy and appreciate them, and I respect that opinion. For me, knowing a wildflower's name matters just as knowing the name of any friend matters. But I admit this philosophy has its limits. One wildflower expert told us she often refers to individual members of the composite family, the numerous hard-to-identify fall asters and yellow daisy-like flowers, as "ADC—another damn composite!"

The opening of the wildflower shop gave Gourdcraft Originals new energy and publicity. Sales were pretty good for a tiny establishment in the middle of nowhere, and the success of our wholesale T-shirt business was making it possible for us to reduce the number of craft fairs we attended. The birth of Blue Creek Valley designs and the new shop also moved our dream along. We now saw the gourd business in the context of a larger vision that emerged as we began to imagine a complex of nature-related shops, each employing a distinct theme and featuring an educational component. I have a memory of one particular walk in the Campbells' pasture when the two of us talked about the way dreams evolve, parting the waters ahead and allowing people to see new possibilities.

To communicate our changing perspective we placed new signs at our entrance. The large sign across the top read *Blue Creek Valley*; under it was a smaller individual one for *Gourdcraft Originals* and another for *Wildflowers*. Thus we were setting the stage for other shops that might someday emerge as part of Blue Creek Valley.

Sometime in 1988 I started to make refrigerator magnet characters called "gourd guys" that became personifications of the foolish gourd life. Though not all were egg-shaped, they looked roughly like Humpty Dumpty with gourd bodies and fabric arms and legs, each of which contained a magnet. We sent my parents the first prototype of a gourd guy as a cheer-up gift and also sent an early model to Janice's grandparents, who called it "the village idiot."

Before the advent of the gourd guys I had discarded several other intriguing ideas that seemed too labor-intensive to be profitable. On first consideration the gourd guy appeared to be another example of such a

Gourdheads pose around a new sign for a publicity shot

losing concept. How could we possibly clean the gourd; burn a face on it and varnish it; sew four tiny sleeves; turn each one inside out so the seam wouldn't show; put a magnet inside each limb; and somehow attach the sleeves to the body—all for the $5 or $6 that people would expect to pay for a refrigerator magnet? It seemed to be an impossible task, but Janice and I both liked the idea too much to give it up. Janice, always a good predictor of the public, knew the magnet people would be popular with customers.

It was all about focus. I learned to sew the tiny sleeves in large numbers, devised a tool for turning them inside out, and eventually found a

Emory Jones

Gourd guys

way to attach the sleeves that our imitators have found hard to duplicate. With a little practice we were able to produce the items somewhat profitably in large numbers, and they proved to be popular as Janice had predicted. Our success with the engineering of gourd guys taught me some valuable lessons as an artist and a human being. Now I try to be receptive to impossible ideas, because often they are the very ones I need to pursue for personal or artistic reasons.

My mother had given me her old sewing machine years before, but I rarely used it until the gourd guys came along. As I rediscovered the pleasure of sewing, I fell in love again with the machine Mama had bought in 1950, the year I was born, and on which she had sewn most of my sister's and my clothes during our childhood. Now losing the use of her hands because of ALS and unable to sew on her modern machine, she tried to give me the newer one, but I didn't want it. I loved the old black Singer

John Kollock

Gourd roping event during the Great Gourd Round-up and Rodeo

and the memories it brought back: of the peaceful feeling its clacking had given me as a child; of importantly threading the needle for Mama when she first began to need reading glasses; of following her around in fabric stores and soaking up the artistic energy in her wake.

Janice and I still enjoy making the gourd guys, which have evolved from bald, generic gourd people into an assortment of male and female characters wearing cowboy hats, baseball caps, straw hats with flowers, and even medical-green scrubs. We like choosing wild and crazy fabrics for some of them that we'd never have the nerve to wear ourselves. Children visiting our shop love to play with the magnet people, making them dance, do acrobatics, and form parades. Adults enjoy using them on refrigerators and filing cabinets as mood indicators. "If my gourd gal is upside down, it means 'watch out,'" one lady told me.

ꙮ

When harvesting time in January 1989 arrived Leon had yet another large crop on the ground, and Janice and I had good crops in our two small patches as well. Our early disastrous attempts at growing gourds seemed far behind us.

This time we staged the Great Gourd Round-up and Rodeo. Our invitation, which featured a drawing of a cowboy roping a gourd, called for entries in a horse show to be held as part of the evening program. About twenty GAGG members made stick horses with gourd heads in advance of the show, which was held in the gymnasium of Cleveland's new primary school. Amazing creativity and wit were displayed as entrants of all ages walked and trotted their mounts around our makeshift arena. The rodeo also included gourd roping and other events that were officiated by Janice, Carey, and me, dressed as rodeo clowns. Everyone took home a bandana with gourd patterns printed on it.

The GAGG spirit was especially vibrant that year. As before, I had some difficulty celebrating such a wonderful occasion with the knowledge that my parents in Savannah were struggling moment by moment to keep their spirits up. By this time Mama was very seriously handicapped, unable to walk at all and steadily losing the use of her arms. Yet it seemed important to affirm life, even in the shadow that ALS had cast over us.

Carpe Diem

In the spring of 1989 Janice and I seized another opportunity to thumb our noses at despair when we heard about an upcoming Fourth of July river parade in the nearby tourist town of Helen. Anyone who wanted to decorate inner tubes or other floats could enter the parade. The storied Chattahoochee River, which originates near the Appalachian Trail in extreme northern White County, runs right through Helen.

I had always wanted an excuse to make a gourd raft. Besides, Janice and I had just seen the movie *Dead Poets' Society*, the theme of which was *carpe diem*, or "seize the day." What better way to seize the day than to make a gourd raft and ride it in a river parade? Janice wanted to be my support crew but wouldn't have any part of being in the parade.

Never was there any question in my mind about whether I could succeed in making a floating gourd vehicle. My main concern was whether there would be enough water in the river for a good ride; the level was usually low in midsummer. Putting that worry aside, I set about finding the best method of gourd raft construction.

I knew on some level that the gourds needed to be contained in a net; but using a net seemed a little like cheating. Determined as usual to do things the hard way, I wanted a pioneer, bare-gourd kind of raft. We had on hand a dozen long, slender gourds about the size of baseball bats that

I lashed together, Huck Finn style, as though they were logs. It was a beautiful raft, but I decided I'd better make a second prototype before going to the river for test rides. Raft number two consisted of nine roundish gourds about eight inches in diameter—three rows of three—connected with hooks and screw eyes.

At 7:00 on a blackberry winter morning in May, Janice and I took the two rafts to Helen for a trial run on the river. I knew the water would be frigid that early in the morning, but I didn't want people to see me making a fool of myself while trying to seize the day. My hope was that no one would be out that early.

Two inches of rain had fallen the day before, and the river looked deeper and swifter than I had anticipated. Janice and I stood on the bank holding the Huck Finn raft, the length of which was almost my height, and tried to figure out how to get me into the water with it. Finally I just threw myself headlong into the river while holding the raft in front of me. The raft fell apart the second it hit the water. Gourds went everywhere, and I sank into an icy, gurgling chaos. I managed to gain my footing in time to recover some of the free-floating gourds and throw them onto the riverbank. Janice helped me out of the river and wrapped a big towel around my goose-pimpled, shivering body.

We found a shallow spot a little farther upstream from which to launch the second raft. I eased it into the current and lay down on it. I can't say the boat was comfortable, but it worked surprisingly well at first. I had a thrilling little ride on it for maybe 25 yards before going through a small rapid and losing half of the raft. The hooks and eyes pulled out of the gourd walls under the pressure of the swiftly moving water. I was cold and discouraged, but those brief moments of success made me want to try again.

That afternoon I went to the hardware store in search of netting. As always, my efforts to explain my project were embarrassing, but a couple of the clerks had become accustomed to my strange schemes by this time. The store didn't sell nets, but one creative clerk had the idea of using a nylon net hammock. I took one home, bagged up about 20 gourds in it, tied it securely, and tried to believe that raft number three would work.

Meanwhile another idea had come to mind that was elegant in its simplicity. Instead of making a complicated raft, why not just *ride on one gourd*, the largest gourd we owned? Maybe I had been making the task more difficult than it needed to be. Our champion gourd grown by Leon

Priscilla riding Gourdzilla during the Helen tube parade

Carter, bigger in cubic inches than a bushel basket, was roughly pear-shaped and as broad at its widest point as the back of a horse. I couldn't wait to ride it.

Back to the raging, frigid river we went, again early in the morning. This time Janice and I took the hammock raft, the bushel gourd, and a life preserver. We'd both realized after the first test rides that I could very well have lost my whole life trying to seize one day. I put the big gourd in the water first and struggled to mount my horse, which turned out to be a cross between a bucking bronco and a greased pig. The gourd would have held me up easily had I only been able to stay on it.

Janice finally stopped laughing long enough to hoist the bronco out of the water and hand me the huge hammock raft. It was even harder to mount. Finally I heaved myself onto it stomach first and went for a short and uncomfortable ride with the unwieldy package of gourds getting snagged or wedged between rocks every few feet.

The date of the parade was getting closer. I had to get serious about making a boat that would take me the distance sitting upright. I bought an additional hammock and did the job right, this time encasing a row of six basketball-sized gourds in each hammock, pea-pod-style, and wrapping the nets tightly around the gourds so that they couldn't move. I then tied the two pods together at each end so that my raft was shaped like a little boat. It didn't have a bottom, but the sides were close enough together so that I was able to sit atop the boat. I was filled with anticipation as we headed once more for the river at 7:00 a.m. This time the raft worked beautifully, and I couldn't stop grinning. *"Carpe diem,"* I whispered to myself as I swirled through the laughing rapids.

Janice later pointed out that, while *I* might think the boat was wonderful, it wasn't very showy. She suggested that I give it a head and call it "Gourdzilla the Sea Serpent," which I did to great effect. After making myself a gourd helmet, I was ready for the parade, which turned out to be fun but a little anticlimactic. My raft went largely unnoticed in the jumble of decorated inner tubes, the occupants of which were busy negotiating the rapids. But Gourdzilla and I did go the distance—and I knew there would be other gourd boats to come.

gourd girls

John Kollock

Art and the Honor System

On a personal level Janice and I were slowly emerging from our cocoon in the late 80s. We both became active in the newly formed White County League of Women Voters and made friends with some very fine women, most of whom were a generation ahead of us. They welcomed us warmly and made us feel needed and appreciated, soon asking each of us to serve as officers and committee members.

I also volunteered to serve on our county's Land Use Planning Committee. The state of Georgia had mandated that every county appoint a group of citizens to draft a land use plan. My participation on this committee was significant for Janice and me in that it caused us to focus on our own plans for relocating someday. We were happy at the Campbell farm and wanted to buy a few acres of it, but the Campbells didn't intend to sell any of their land. So, with the knowledge that our choice of a permanent business location could be limited by future zoning regulations, we began keeping our eyes open for a new business home.

That "wake-up call" about zoning was to be an important catalyst for us, but our concern turned out to be quite premature. Ironically, 15 years later White County still has no zoning ordinances.

Janice and I were also receiving regular invitations from from civic and garden clubs to give presentations about our business, and these experiences helped us to feel more a part of the community at large. We prepared a slide show and took turns narrating it, sharing much of our gourd humor in the process. These programs were well received, and we always had a sense that there were people in the audience thinking, "Gee, the gourd girls don't seem weird at all! They're nice, personable folks!"

We were still closeted during this time—which is to say we probably could have named and counted on our fingers every person to whom we had come out, swearing each to secrecy.

❧

It was in 1989 that Janice first visited Nacoochee Presbyterian Church (NPC). For several years we'd heard about this small congregation that, committed to social and environmental justice, offered "old hippies" and other progressive types a church community. The close-knit congregation at Nacoochee drew many baby boomers who hadn't been to church in years, among them GAGG members and other friends of ours. For Janice, who'd grown up as a Presbyterian and had begun to wish for a church connection, NPC seemed like the place to be.

It was only a 15-minute drive in linear time from our home in Blue Creek to the church, but in metaphorical time the distance was light years. The church is located in the northern part of our county in the tiny community called Sautee-Nacoochee, named for the two enchanting valleys that dovetail there. "The valleys," as most residents call this geographical area, have always had a special aura about them. Who can say why certain places on this earth feel sacred? I believe that beautiful, peaceful places can focus human attention on the Creative Force and thus intensify our awareness of it.

Artists especially have always been drawn to areas where natural beauty provides subject matter and inspiration; thus a gradual influx of artistic people over the last 200 years undoubtedly had helped to foster an attitude of open-mindedness as well as reverence among the people of the valleys. The result was a pocket of our county that had become known over time for its high concentration of outlanders and artists, intellectuals and freethinkers.

Nacoochee Presbyterian Church, along with other organizations in this unique community, continues to honor the tradition of reverence, creativity, and open-mindedness established over the years. NPC is housed in a 75-year-old small white frame building in the heart of the

Sautee-Nacoochee community. Its simplicity of design speaks of a quiet faith tradition that doesn't require ornamentation or approval from outside to be sure of who it is.

At the time Janice began visiting NPC, Rev. John Hobbs had been the pastor for only a year but was clearly a good match with the community. A handsome, clean-cut man around 40, John was married to Esther White Hobbs, with whom he had two young children. He was a feminist, a strong advocate for racial minorities, and an exceptionally sweet-natured, nurturing person. Janice and John, who was about my age of 39, hit it off instantly. He began visiting our shop and made friends with both of us, as did Esther.

Soon Janice was ready to join the church—but she wanted to come out to John before doing so. He was very welcoming and made it clear to both of us that social justice for gay and lesbian people was important to him. Although I was pleased for Janice, I wasn't sure whether even the "granola church," as some people called NPC, was for me. In January of 1990 I visited there and wrote in my journal:

> I went to church yesterday for the first time—other than
> with family—in 15 years or so. The people at Nacoochee
> Presbyterian are really good—friendly, accepting, down
> to earth. In a way I think I'd enjoy being part of the
> fellowship . . . but I wonder if my beliefs have drifted
> too far from traditional Christian theology.

The question of church attendance was largely a moot one for me since I traveled to Savannah to see my parents on many weekends when they were not at their mountain cabin. In fact, my growing preoccupation with my parents' struggle was a factor in Janice's need for a church community. She joined the church on a Sunday in the early spring of 1990 when I was in Savannah, and we both felt sad about my absence from this important event. I began to go to NPC with her more often when I was in town and to wonder how I would fit into Janice's new community.

❧

Our energy for the business remained strong in spite of my frequent trips to Savannah. We introduced new wildflower designs each spring and fall and began trying to build a retail mail-order business, producing a couple

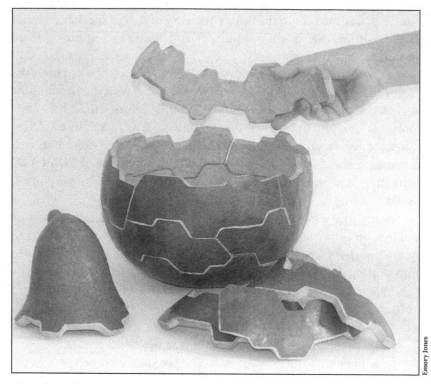

Gourd puzzle

of costly color brochures that didn't pay off for us. We soon saw that success in the mail-order business required more capital and business know-how than we had at our disposal. Meanwhile the wholesale shirt business was still doing well.

I continued to push myself artistically, partly because I still enjoyed the challenge of developing new ways to use gourds and partly because I was fearful of having friends and customers think my work was becoming tired and humdrum. True to my seventh grade history teacher's characterization of me as "Yogi Berra the pinch-hitter," I performed best under pressure.

One of my all-time favorite concepts was the gourd puzzle. Choosing an exceptionally sturdy and balanced gourd, I would carve a simple horizontal design on it and then cut the gourd in layers, each layer having tabs that fit into the next. Putting the puzzle together meant rebuilding the original gourd. This concept was an apt expression of the artistic

John Kollock

Woven gourds

possibilities presented by a three-dimensional, hollow object. Current visitors to The Gourd Place still enjoy a puzzle that we keep in the shop for their entertainment.

Basketry was another realm I explored around the same time period. I made gourd frames by cutting dozens of pieces out in a pattern and then weaving in reed or other natural materials. Other artists have used gourds as bases for baskets, but my concept is different, incorporating the basketry materials into the gourd's natural shape and thus maintaining the integrity of the gourd.

An even more labor-intensive type of basket I've made gives the illusion of a woven vessel. Dozens of small squares are cut, allowing the gourd itself to represent the weaving material. The illusion is created by carving or burning lines to indicate the over-and-under weaving pattern.

During the late 1980s, even though our shop was officially open only on Saturdays and Sundays, we had a few people stopping by on weekdays. At times when we were away, we began using an honor system so people could come in and enjoy the shop without our being there. We made a sign instructing anyone wanting to make a purchase to list the items they were buying, figure their sales tax on a pad we provided, and deposit their

John Kollock

Illusion basket

money in a large gourd bank with a slot in the side. The gourd had a lock that prevented the lid from being opened, but of course someone could easily enough have taken the entire gourd and broken it open. No one did. People were unfailingly honest, appreciative of our trust, and amused at the novelty of such an arrangement. A few of our visitors still talk about the old honor system.

Most weekdays Janice, Carey, and I were in the workshop. We left the retail building across the way unlocked but used an old-fashioned gas-station alert system to let us know when we had a visitor. Any time a car drove over the rubber hose in the driveway, a bell rang loudly in the workshop and one of us went over to play hostess.

Unbeknownst to us, we had one regular visitor who didn't trip the bell because she was on foot: June Morris, a neighbor who had moved to Blue Creek with her husband, Bill, in 1980. The Morrises lived half a mile down a pretty dirt lane, but their mailbox was out on the highway next to the Campbell property. June walked to the box every day and, if the postal carrier hadn't come, often spent a few minutes looking around our shop while she waited for the mail.

After the opening of our wildflower shop Janice and I had begun taking some of our daily walks on the Morrises' road instead of in the pasture because so many native plants bloomed along their roadside. There were bellwort, spiderwort, wild geranium, two kinds of trillium, a rare plant called monkshood, and easily a dozen more. We sometimes walked after lunch, the same time June went to get her mail, and occasionally met her on the road. We asked permission to pick flowers from her property for our "Now in Bloom" display in the wildflower shop, and she graciously consented. Soon the three of us were having friendly chats when we ran into each other.

June laughingly confessed her habit of "sneaking" past our driveway alarm and told us how much she enjoyed the shop. A Mississippi native in her 50s, she had auburn hair, a redhead's complexion, and a wonderful sense of humor.

In the spring of 1990 Janice and I asked June if she would like to fill in as a shopkeeper from time to time. She soon became an important part of our lives. Her delightful way of finding and expressing the humor in almost any situation endeared her to us from the start. Always poking good-natured fun at human nature in general and herself in particular, she loved interacting with visitors and telling us the funny things she and they said. One of the best was her account of a conversation with a woman who couldn't seem to understand that gourd seeds were inside of gourds, but instead thought the whole gourd was a seed. "Well, my land," June imitated her, pointing to a gourd as large as a beach ball, "you'd have to dig a mighty big hole to plant that 'un!"

At the time June first started helping us, I needed all the laughs I could get, overwhelmed as I was by my mother's illness. She helped to see us through the last year of Mama's life with her support and her willingness to work on weekends occasionally so Janice could go to Savannah with me.

We were to see each other through more good and bad times. Eventually when Janice and I came out as a couple to June and her husband, Bill, we were blessed by their easy acceptance of us and their continuing friendship.

🌰

Our longtime friend and helper Carey Kollock left us in 1990. Always a great animal lover, she found a job as a veterinarian's assistant. Though we were sad to see her go, we knew the job would be perfect for her.

It was almost no time after Carey left that Patty Workman stopped by the shop and expressed an interest in helping us. In her late 20s at the time, she was a pretty person with longish light brown hair and smiling green eyes. We had met Patty previously through a mutual friend and knew her to be bright, friendly, and artistically talented; we offered her a job on the spot. She was enthusiastic, hard-working and very knowledgeable about wildflowers as well. Patty quickly learned Carey's many different jobs—cleaning, dyeing, varnishing, and cutting the gourds, among others—and was soon an integral part of the gourd life.

Hard Times and New Horizons

Concern for both my parents' well-being claimed more and more of my energy as Mama's physical deterioration continued relentlessly. Although Janice and I both derived much pleasure from our business and the success of the wildflower shirts, our pace was quite stressful at times, especially in combination with my family situation. I found comfort in our peaceful home and surroundings.

My parents came to their cabin late in the spring of 1990 and stayed until the end of July. Mama was now unable to do anything for herself, and it was clear that this would be her last trip to the mountains. Daddy was an unbelievably devoted and cheerful caregiver but carried a tremendous load. I wanted to do as much as possible to help him as well as Mama while they were nearby, as did Janice. We spent much time at the cabin with them after working hours. I wrote in my journal:

> I do as much for Mama as I can—feed her, brush her teeth, wash her face, etc. Sometimes we laugh together when she sees me making weird, unconscious faces while giving her a bite or brushing her teeth. Sometimes she cries and tells me how sweet and gentle I am. I want to give her the kind of loving care she gave me as a child. Her voice is getting weaker

and her articulation worse—I hope the day won't come when she can't be understood.

That day did come. Victims of ALS, while remaining mentally sharp, usually lose their ability to talk as well as write, and become tragically unable to communicate their thoughts and needs. Of all the indignities and difficulties Mama faced, our eventual inability to understand what she tried to say was most painful for her and for her loved ones.

At the end of July I helped my parents make the trip back to Savannah. Because Mama's condition had deteriorated so much during the summer, we were all especially fearful about how hard the eight-hour journey would be for her. They had bought a van with a lift, but she was very uncomfortable sitting in her wheelchair for long periods of time. At first she had been able to sit in the passenger seat in the front of the van, but now she couldn't sit up well enough to ride there safely.

So we propped several large pillows on one end of the back seat, and I sat close to Mama to support her on her other side. This worked fairly well, but we were both cramped, and I was extremely anxious about her comfort and state of mind the entire trip. In an effort to calm myself and be positive, I began singing an old tune called "Smooth Sailing" inside my head and kept the refrain going as background music off and on during the trip:

> We've got smooth sailing, sailing . . .
> Looks like every drop of rain is gone, gone, gone,
> Smooth sailing, sailing,
> And a blue sky full of rainbows from now on.
> *(Song by Sonny Throckmorton and Curly Putnan)*

I'm not a sailor and had never thought about sailing as a metaphor for getting through hard times; but for some reason that song helped me in those hours. The refrain, which foreshadowed future events, came back often during the months that followed and still comes back to me regularly.

Soon after making that last trip home with my parents, I began driving to Savannah every two weeks. More than ever, I was torn between responsibilities to my parents, to Janice, and to our business. Mama and Daddy were never demanding—quite the opposite—and appreciated whatever help my sister, Nancy, and I could give them. Nancy lived in Raleigh and alternated weekends with me. Our brother, Bill, lived in Washington state and thus was unable to come often.

Some bright spots for me during those trips were visits with my grandmother Mae Mae, who lived in Thomson, about halfway between home and Savannah. I always stopped to visit her, even if only for a short while. She and Granddaddy, who had been dead many years, had retired in the early 1960s to the shaded little white Victorian house with dark green shutters that had been the last home of Mae Mae's parents. The front door opened into a wide entry hall with a beautiful heart pine floor. The parlor on the right still looked as it had in the 1920s with portraits of mysterious ancestors on the walls and a crazy quilt draped over the back of the wine-colored velvet settee.

The room opposite the parlor, where Mae Mae and I sat when I visited, was a cozy den. Now 91 and getting frail, Mae Mae still had her trademark *joie de vivre* and was more than ever an inspiration to me. At least once I asked her to tell me the secret to her magic way of being. My directness made her a little uncomfortable, but she tried to oblige me: "I just try to be good company," she said simply. As we parted, she never failed to say, "Now give my little Janice a big hug for me!"

Mae Mae and I called each other on the telephone often during that period. Her vision was failing, and she had large numerals on her phone so that she could see to dial. Once when Janice and I went through the drive-in window at our bank in Cleveland, the teller said to me, laughing, "Your grandmother asked me to have you call her!" In response to my confused look, she explained that Mae Mae had dialed a wrong number the night before—that just happened to be the teller's—and had struck up a conversation with her. "Do you know my little granddaughter who has the gourd business?" Mae Mae had asked, and the teller had replied that she did. When I called Mae Mae that night, she didn't seem at all surprised. "Did the little girl from the bank give you my message?" she asked.

🦃

As my work on White County's Land Use Planning Committee continued, Janice and I became more and more concerned about finding a new location for our business in case zoning ordinances were to be enacted. In a last effort to make the Campbell place our permanent home, we had the farmhouse and three acres appraised and made Mr. and Mrs. Campbell a good offer, but they turned us down. They were committed to keeping the property all in one piece, and we understood their position.

In the fall of 1990 Mildred Neville found the place that would become our new location for Gourdcraft Originals. Mildred, who'd always enjoyed looking at property for sale, took us to see an 11-acre tract with two houses on Duncan Bridge Road, which runs perpendicular to Blue Creek Road. Though Janice and I had passed the place countless times on our way to Sautee-Nacoochee and points north, from the road we'd had no inkling of how lovely the property was.

From the road we had seen only a couple of plain-Jane houses painted a pea-green color and surrounded by suburban-looking boxwoods. But when we pulled into the driveway, went up a little rise, and parked near the buildings, we saw another world below us. A grassy slope behind the two houses led down to a beautiful pond. Two large magnolias and two large willows—the only trees that Janice and I had talked about wanting on our dream property—dominated the landscape. The property looked and felt like a park, a perfect setting for the retail nature center we envisioned. We walked around the lake, which was grassy on the left side and woodsy on the right. From the dam on the back side of the lake we saw Mount Yonah and its reflection in the water.

We later learned from the real estate agent that the property had been the retirement home of Henry and Ann Cobb until Henry's death a couple of years before. Mrs. Cobb eventually had moved to an assisted living facility in Atlanta to be near her son. Their former residence seemed well suited for use as retail and museum space and had a roomy basement for storage. The small guest cottage next door would be ideal for a workshop. Everything was perfect except the price, which was way beyond our reach.

Janice was in love. I liked the place as well but, always the financial conservative of the pair, didn't think we should be mooning over something we couldn't have. The amount of property, number of buildings, and asking price were all twice what we had in mind. And I was living in a fog of worry and grief, unable to get into my old dreaming mode. We put our thoughts of a move on the back burner.

&

In early December of 1990 Janice went with me for a visit to Savannah. After we returned home I wrote:

Mama is so weak and uncomfortable, but she tries to be

John Kollock

View of Yonah from east side of the lake

cheerful and sweet-natured and does amazingly well at it. I feel love, forgiveness, tenderness for her like I would never have felt under other circumstances; yet the pain of watching them suffer seems unbearable when I'm with them. I fear too for Daddy's health and safety.

The very next day I had a call from Savannah. Daddy had had a mild heart attack and was scheduled for triple bypass surgery the next morning. I flew down that night and along with my sister, Nancy, spent several difficult weeks trying to nurture both of our parents after Daddy's surgery.

Janice stayed home and kept our business going during this period with the help of Patty Workman and June Morris. Her friends at Nacoochee Presbyterian were also very supportive and even offered to help her mind the shop in my absence; her bond with the church grew stronger. The two of us talked on the phone daily, but usually someone was around to hear my end of the conversation; so I had to be guarded in what I could say to her. My inability to talk naturally to my spouse made the separation even more difficult for both of us.

Daddy was making a good recovery from his surgery, but he could no longer lift and care for Mama as he had done before. He began employing around-the-clock aides to help with her care, and Nancy and I went back to alternating our weekend visits to Savannah. We were able to help in many ways and to bolster our parents' spirits, but neither of us was physically strong enough to lift Mama. Our lives revolved around the schedules of several strong, loving women who cared for her. Her condition went from as bad as seemed possible to worse and still worse. I think all of us felt we would drown in interminable grief and hopelessness. We coped, as families do, by going through the motions of life and honoring an unspoken agreement not to verbalize the depths of our despair to one another. There were tears and expressions of love, but the deepest pain we kept to ourselves.

gourd girls

Odd-yssey

$\mathcal{S}$omehow we staged another gourd gathering in January 1991. The theme was Beyond the Gourd Earth: A Space Odd-yssey. In view of my parents' situation the timing couldn't have been worse, but we had hundreds of gourds in Leon's field to be gathered before the rats and squirrels damaged them. And, as before, Janice and I were intentional about having the party as a way of affirming life in the face of ALS. Patty, always cheerful and upbeat, helped us immeasurably in that resolve.

On the surface the event seemed as fun and funky as ever, but I think many of us sensed that our gourd gathering days were numbered if not at an end. Leon Carter had mentioned that he was ready to stop farming, and before the year was out he sold his four acres of bottomland. We had harvested our last crop beside Blue Creek.

Changes of all kinds, good and bad, came fast that year. Janice's regular route between our house and Nacoochee Church took her down Duncan Bridge Road past the Cobb property that we had not pursued because of the price. Thus the place was never far from her thoughts. One day she noticed that the real estate agent's sign had been replaced by a "For sale by owner" sign. She wanted to find out if the asking price had come down. Though she understood the pressures and grief I was coping with, Janice felt a strong sense of urgency about trying to buy the

Rob Smith as a three-headed alien during one of the Space Odd-yssey skits

property against all odds. She reminded me frequently that our lives mattered, that we had to think about moving forward.

My head knew she was right, but my heart pleaded to be left alone, to be spared the additional stress of contemplating such a huge financial and emotional leap. In the end what prevailed was my need to prove to Janice—and myself—that I could still muster some interest in our life and future together.

We eventually met with Hart Cobb, the son of owner Ann Cobb, whom we liked a great deal. The asking price had come down considerably, and owner-financing was a possibility. The Cobbs knew the property was valuable and could eventually have brought a higher price, but they also cared deeply about its future and didn't want it to be turned into an RV park. Hart liked our nature center concept and saw us as good caretakers of the tremendous investment of love that his mother and late father had made in their special place.

Janice and I approached one bank about financing, just to test the waters. After analyzing the information we provided, the bankers told us the purchase would be too much of a stretch for us. We decided to buy anyway, basing our decision on dreams, on the willingness of the Cobbs to finance the sale, and on the generous offer of my sister and brother-in-law, Nancy and Ned Nutt, to lend us money for a down payment. On paper the purchase was definitely not a good move, but then the idea of a gourd business had never looked good on paper in the first place.

We didn't know whether we'd be able to manage payments on two properties, but we wanted to continue living in our dream house in Blue Creek. So much of us was in that house, and we had had only a few years to enjoy it. We decided to keep our residence and commute to work for the first time since being self-employed. The house would be our "ace in the hole," our hedge against possible financial difficulties ahead. If the load proved to be more than we could manage, we would sell the house and move into the guest cottage on the business property.

We met Ann Cobb for the first time at the closing around the first of March. A slight woman whose sweetness spilled out in her every look and word, she was starting to suffer with memory problems—but she had no trouble recalling how much she and her late husband had loved the place she was entrusting to us. "Henry and I used to sit on the back porch looking out on the lake and watching the deer or the wild ducks," she told us brightly, "and argue about which one of us loved our place the most!"

John Kollock's smart idea eight years earlier to construct our retail building with a future move in mind would soon become a reality. We began making arrangements to move it to the new property, but we had trouble deciding exactly where to locate it in relation to the existing main house and guest cottage. We imagined various configurations that would allow visitors to move easily from one building to the next, but the only placement that seemed aesthetically pleasing was adjacent to the back corner of the main house. From this spot it would offer a view of the lake and would not, we hoped, appear crowded too close to the other building.

I called my grandmother Mae Mae, who was visiting my aunt in Atlanta at the time, and told her all about the new place, including our difficulty in deciding where to locate the building. Excited in spite of feeling a little apprehensive for us, she wanted to see the property for herself, so she and my aunt planned to come for the day on March 5.

On the Sunday afternoon of March 4, Janice and I were minding the store when Daddy called to tell us that Mae Mae had had a massive heart attack. We made it to the hospital in Decatur in time to be with her that evening. Still focused outside herself as she had always been, she wanted to advise us about the move. "Dahlins, don't crowd your buildings," she told us weakly. When we left her we were trying our best to believe her condition would improve and that we'd see her the next day. I walked away from her backwards, smiling at her and memorizing her face. She died in the night.

For the first hours after learning of Mae Mae's death, I felt panicky. I saw the two of us standing on either side of a glass wall; I could feel her near me but couldn't reach her. I spent much of the first two days after her death mentally pressed up against that glass wall pleading for her to come to me or say something to me. She said only a few words in a soothing but firm voice: "It's all right, dahlin." As the days went by the image and my Mae Mae receded further and further from me.

Janice was seated with our family at Mae Mae's funeral service but was not beside me as I would have wanted. Taking the initiative to have her sit next to me would have been unthinkable, because such an act in my mind would have been a step out of the closet. Mostly I was numbly grateful that she was seated with the family. Mae Mae and Janice had loved each other like grandmother and granddaughter.

Mae Mae had asked in her will that a newspaper column I'd written about her be read at her funeral. Her request for the reading meant everything to me, for she'd apparently believed that I had spoken the truth about her wonderful way with people:

> Most people seem to think that Mae Mae and others who know her secrets are lucky to be the way they are. I'm here to tell you that I know and love one of these magic people very well and have watched her closely; and I say there's little luck involved. Her gift, like any other talent, is the result of love, work, and discipline.

Don't Roll Back

Around the end of March we paid off the note on our building at the Campbell farm and moved it down the road. We had decided to place it adjacent to the back of the existing main house, hoping Mae Mae would have approved.

Mae Mae left each of her grandchildren a small sum of money, and mine was spent on constructing a combination ramp and walkway between the two buildings as well as painting the guest cottage and main house dark green. Since the time 14 years before when she'd bought us a refrigerator to help us set up housekeeping in the Campbells' farmhouse, Mae Mae had regularly given her approval and her dollars. Now for the last time she had contributed financially and spiritually to the business and life Janice and I were creating together. Two rocking chairs from her front porch, now on the back porch of our main building, are a constant reminder of her presence.

I made a videotape to show my parents the spectacle of the shop being moved down the road and the new property. I wondered whether they were as sadly puzzled as I was by my ability to carry out this move while they were living such a hellish existence, but I wanted to include them in what was happening. As we watched the tape together they were as engaged as they could have been under the circumstances. Mama had

John Kollock

Our building in its new location, with the main house on the left

been anxious about the load of financial stress we were assuming, but her personal struggle left little room even for the habitual worrying about her children that had always been part of her life. She fell asleep watching the tape, and I found an odd comfort in that.

During that visit I wrote in my journal:

> This is such a strange time—of the interminable suffering with Mama and preparing for her death; of struggling with Daddy as he tries to regain his *joie de vivre* against strong odds; of losing my beautiful Mae Mae. And yet it is a time for a new beginning, a new chapter in the experiment that became a dream. Life for us is not only going on; it is expanding and demanding in the face of death. And—the dead and dying are very much a part of this life, this dream.

During that spring I began to pray constantly for an end to my mother's suffering. On the night of May 31, three nights after my last visit, she died in her sleep. Everyone who loved her felt a strange melding of peace and sorrow at her passing. Her memorial service was a tribute not only to Mama but also to the many people who had supported her for so long. I had grown close to my parents' devoted friends and to the women employed to take care of her in the last months of her life.

Like others who have lost loved ones to slow death, I was surprisingly unprepared for the loss when it finally came. And along with grieving for my mother herself, I grieved for the fact that our relationship, however close, had been incomplete. She would never know the truth that was the source of my greatest joy and pain all rolled into one: my love for Janice. There was some comfort in the knowledge that, from Mama's point of view, she *had* known me through and through—and that she had been spared the difficulty our coming out would have brought her. Still, I felt cheated.

I tried to keep those feelings at bay along with deepening questions about the wisdom of our recent property purchase; it felt as though a huge load of grief and fear would come crashing in on me if I let down my guard for a moment. Then I heard a comforting message in my mother's voice one time in those early days after her death, just as I had heard Mae Mae's.

Mama used to tell a funny story about her first driving test. Driving a car with a clutch—the only kind that existed in the 1940s—with the examiner beside her, she found herself stopped for a red light at the top of the only steep hill in Orlando, Florida. The examiner instructed her to turn the engine off and start it back up from this difficult position. She tried and failed a couple of times, and then a school bus full of children came up behind her. The young examiner, who had been all professionalism up to that point, completely lost his cool and yelled at Mama over and over, *"Don't roll back, lady, please don't roll back!"* Finally Mama put on the emergency brake and got out of the car. "You drive the damn thing!" she said to the instructor. Needless to say, she didn't get her license that day, but she always enjoyed telling that story.

So when I heard my mother's voice one evening as I struggled internally to keep up the momentum that I desperately needed, her laughing words were *"Don't roll back, lady, don't roll back!"*

❧

On a Saturday in June of 1991 we held the grand opening of our new location with the help of our Foothills Guild friends, who agreed to come and exhibit their art on the grounds. The event, which had been planned months ahead of time, came just two weeks after Mama's death. Daddy drove up from Savannah for the weekend to see our property and to be with us for the occasion. As I showed him around we talked tearfully about our wish that Mama could have been part of this new chapter in the gourd life.

Beside the flagstone walkway that led from the parking area to the main building, visitors on grand opening day found a sign that illustrated our long-range plan for the property. An enlarged plat showed where future nature trails and shop buildings would be located. Under it was printed our newly created mission statement:

> GOURDCRAFT ORIGINALS AND COMPANY
> *nature specialty shops*
> Our purpose is to combine nature-oriented
> retail shops and educational exhibits
> in a unique way by creating a park where people
> can learn about nature while supporting
> the project economically.

Janice and I knew the retail nature center concept was innovative, worthwhile, meant-to-be. but we didn't know how to make it happen without capital. The key to its implementation would be finding several merchants who would create shops around specific nature themes, provide related educational opportunities for visitors, and collaborate with us in promoting the attraction. But because our property, however lovely and well suited to the purpose, was not on the beaten path for tourists, we weren't comfortable trying to convince anyone to take a risk until our number of visitors grew.

So we put our concept out into the universe in the form of the mission statement at our entrance and hoped—in retrospect, I think irrationally—that visitors would become excited about the venture and thus help to make it happen with their positive energy. I have no idea whether many people understood or were drawn to the concept. The few who commented on it seemed to be missing the point. They thought we were trying to create an artists' community, because that was a model with which they were familiar. The idea of a retail nature center was not familar to most people and therefore did not capture their imaginations.

An exception was longtime close friend, woodworker, and GAGG member Marge Felder, who was excited about the concept. Marge, a petite, spirited woman close to my father's age, had moved to the mountains from Atlanta 10 years before and turned her woodworking hobby into a profession. An unusually capable and enthusiastic person who was as nurturing of her friends' dreams as she was of her own far-ranging ones, she was very supportive of our nature-center vision. Marge opened a shop called *Small Wooden Objects* in one of the rooms in the main building, and in keeping with our mission statement, created an educational display of the kinds of wood she was using. We talked of a future tree identification project as well. Although the nature center as we had first envisioned it never quite materialized, Marge kept her shop with us for about 10 years and helped us make a go of our new venture by paying a small rent, sharing in shopkeeping duties, and continually encouraging us.

In addition, Janice and I decided to open a bird and butterfly shop and called it *Winged Things*. We bought some books and other items on our small budget and put together an exhibit featuring a collection of birds' nests.

The main building now housed our gourd museum and wildflower shop as well as the two new shops. Sliding glass doors on the back side of the large wildflower room, which looked out on the lake, opened onto a small screened porch and a newly constructed wooden walkway to the original gourd shop. From the front of the gourd shop there were steps leading down toward the trail around the lake.

Our grand opening was successful in terms of attendance if not sales. The visitors, including many friends and GAGG members, were happy about our bold move. I believe they thought we were gutsy. I was shaking in my shoes. I felt breathless with excitement and anxiety and confusion, as though I was on a train that would not stop moving for death, grief, or anything else.

❧

One way that I coped with the runaway-train feeling for a time was by walking the four miles from home to work. Complaining that driving to our place of business made me feel like I had a "real job," I realized that walking to work was still an option even though the distance was fairly long. One morning I struck out on foot, and the one-way commute took me a full hour of working time I could ill afford to lose—but I loved it and resolved to indulge myself three times a week.

Having walked for exercise and recreation all my adult life, I now discovered that as a form of transportation it was even more enjoyable.

There was something about moving purposefully through time and space that felt natural and therapeutic. Because a long section of my route was a seldom-traveled dirt road, I was able to lose myself in thought without being jolted back to reality by passing cars. I often imagined the days when a person's feet were his or her only means of transportation. I thought, too, how many present-day pleasures can best be experienced on foot, such as watching the progress of a neighbor's garden, noticing the smell of someone's breakfast drifting from a house, or investigating an unfamiliar wildflower along the roadside.

When I emerged from the dirt road back onto the highway I always experienced a kind of culture shock, but I still took comfort in my ability to choose the slow lane for a few hours a week. I kept up the practice for only six months or so, but it helped me make the transition into a new phase of the gourd life.

gourd girls

Emory Jones

Pure Gold

*I*n September 1991 Janice and I celebrated the 17th anniversary of our life partnership. We were still feeling off balance and smarting from the events of the year, but we were thankful to be enjoying our beautiful place together. Some evenings after we closed the shop we stayed and sat in Mae Mae's rockers on the back porch for our cocktail hour, which for us meant popcorn and beer. As we watched for deer and wild ducks, we imagined Henry and Ann Cobb sitting where we now sat and arguing about which of them loved the place most.

During the time since my mother's death Janice and I had naturally been worried about Daddy. Always an upbeat, optimistic person by nature, he appeared to be coping as well as anyone could after losing his spouse of 49 years. Undecided about where he wanted to live, he remained in Savannah but kept busy traveling and visiting his three grown children. He was with Janice and me for our Foothills Guild holiday open house the first weekend in December, and we asked him to wear a Santa suit and play the role of Gourda Claus during the event. His gourdhead mask had a beard and Santa hat glued to it. Children of all ages loved having their pictures taken with Gourda Claus, and Daddy enjoyed the role. He posed with dozens of people and if nothing else was distracted from his grief for a couple of days.

Bill Wilson as Gourda Claus with, **left to right,** *Patty Workman, June Morris, Janice, and Priscilla*

Two days before Christmas Daddy and I drove together to Raleigh to visit my sister, Nancy, and her family. On the way he told me casually that he had met and dated Berenice Marston from Beaufort, South Carolina. Nancy and I happily took note of the fact that he called her a couple of times while we were there.

Early the following February Daddy brought Berenice to introduce her to his mountain home and to Janice and me. She was an attractive, well-educated woman in her 50s with a great sense of humor. She was easy to know and like. When Daddy brought her to the shop we were pleased to note that she genuinely caught on to the gourd life. Berenice has continued to be one of our most enthusiastic and discerning supporters.

The reason for their visit turned out to be not only an introduction, but also an announcement that they planned to marry the following week in Beaufort. It had been a whirlwind romance, but they were both very happy and sure of what they wanted. Soon after their marriage, they told us, they planned to sell their respective homes in Savannah and Beaufort and to make their permanent home on the property adjoining ours. They would build a new house next door to the cabin.

Janice and I were happy for Daddy and Berenice and pleased that they would become our permanent neighbors, but at the same time we had a panicky feeling. Neither of us could imagine having my father so close while we remained closeted. We were exhausted from years of being on guard and feeling like strangers to our families. And we believed it would be wrong not to come out to Daddy, for he might regret the move later if he learned the truth. I never doubted that he would love me unconditionally but reasoned that he might not want to live close by if he was uncomfortable around us. So we made the decision to come out to Daddy, and Janice immediately blurted, "Well, we're not going to tell your father without telling my mother!" Of course she was right. It was way past time.

Coming out to our parents was the hardest thing we had ever contemplated doing, but we laughed about the fact that, in view of the length and faithfulness of our partnership, no one could claim it was just a passing phase. There wasn't much time to accomplish the task since Daddy and Berenice were already working on house plans. I decided to write Daddy a letter. Though some people may regard this as a cowardly method of coming out, I believe it is often the most humane in that the recipient of the news has time to absorb the information and to think before they have to respond.

Janice wanted to tell her mother, Nancy, in person, and we already had plans to stay with her the following week while exhibiting and selling our wildflower shirts in the Atlanta Flower Show. So I mailed my letter to Daddy a few days before we went to Atlanta and gave him the phone number at Nancy's in case he wanted to call me there.

On the day before the flower show was to begin Janice and I drove into the city, set up our booth display, and went to Nancy's condo in nearby Tucker late that afternoon. We'd barely had time to greet her before Janice said, "Mama, I have something to tell you. Let's have a drink." When the time finally came my partner was gutsy and strong.

By prearrangement I slipped upstairs to give them privacy for the conversation. But it was only a minute before Janice yelled for me to come back down. Nancy accepted the news with grace and equanimity, and the relief Janice and I felt was indescribable. I remember that it was a long while before my hands stopped shaking. Both of us felt as though we'd just barely avoided a terrible automobile accident.

Within the hour Nancy's phone rang, and our hearts began racing all over again. Sure enough, it was Daddy. He told me that everything was okay, that nothing could change his love for me. We didn't talk at great length, but I heard his message of acceptance and cried with relief. Berenice got on the phone and conveyed her warm feelings for us as well. Janice and I were deeply thankful for the fact that she had undoubtedly helped Daddy to deal with the news initially and would continue to be there for him.

The rest of our week in Atlanta passed in a blur. We were exhibiting in the flower show for the fourth time, and our sales had peaked a year or two before. Thus business wasn't great that week, but we didn't care. We sat in our T-shirt booth, grinned at each other, and wondered if we needed to pinch ourselves, so great was our joy. After 17 years together, we now had no secrets from our parents—and they loved us still.

When we returned home, still grinning after the week in Atlanta, one of the first things we wanted to do was walk up on Yonah to the place where my family had scattered my mother's ashes the previous fall. Janice had minded the shop on that October Saturday afternoon and had not been part of the quiet family ritual, so since then she and I had been wanting to go there together.

For the 12 years we'd lived in Blue Creek Janice and I had enjoyed our own private access to the eastern, gently sloping side of Yonah through the back of the Campbells' pasture. We had established a regular route that took us under the pasture fence, through a neighbor's property, and up an old roadbed into national forest land. There we found ourselves in a deeply shaded world of staid old trees and fresh-born wildflowers, ancient boulders and newly sprung, dancing streams of water. It was a paradise for us, children at heart that we were, where we sprawled on mammoth rocks, drank from springs without fear, imagined Native Americans moving about on that nurturing mountain in times past.

On a chilly, overcast February afternoon we made the familiar trek so I could show Janice the place where Mama's ashes had been scattered. I think we both wanted to include her in our amazing experience of coming out to our parents, an experience from which we were still glowing. As we headed up the mountain I hoped I would be able to recognize the spot; the winter had been rainy and windy, and newly fallen trees had changed the landscape considerably.

We approached what I believed to be the right area, a tiny clearing between the roadbed and a particularly pretty stretch of creek. I was startled and amazed to see that some ashes were still visible on the ground after four months and many rains. I pointed them out to Janice, and we stood staring open-mouthed at a small mound of gray-white dust. Suddenly we both felt an overwhelming sense of my mother's presence as a flash of gold came into view atop the pillow of ashes. It was real: a gold band, my mother's wedding band. I am wearing it as I write.

I know that the presence of the ring can be explained in logical terms and that the way it seemed magically to materialize was probably just a result of our eyes focusing. But we understood that Mama was with us in that moment and acknowledged our commitment.

gourd girls

Staying Afloat

The previous fall the nominating committee at Nacoochee Presbyterian Church had asked Janice to serve as an elder. She'd been ordained early in 1992, not long before our coming out to our parents, and had taken on the demanding job with pleasure and dedication. The opportunity to serve her new church community meant a great deal to her.

I attended church with Janice most Sundays now and enjoyed being part of the community as well, though I did not join the church. My long absence from organized religion and the experience of my mother's agonizing death had left me curiously disconnected from the strong faith of my adolescence. I continued to hold to a vague belief in a higher power, or Life Spark, as I called it, but was clueless as to how it might operate in the world or how I should honor it in my life. Still, I enjoyed being at Nacoochee and found comfort and peace in songs and rituals that took me back to my childhood. Although only a few close friends in the congregation knew for sure that we were a couple, Janice and I felt as though most people had us figured out and accepted us. We were comfortable and able to be ourselves at Nacoochee.

The same winter of Janice's ordination the two of us initiated the formation of a readers' theater group at the Sautee-Nacoochee Community Center across the road from the church, where Janice now served on the

Board. I had had an interest in readers' theater since my Auburn University days as a speech minor, and now I focused on the medium again. The happy events of the winter had generated new creative energy for me, and Janice too was enthusiastic about readers' theater. Both of us were ready to stretch our cramped psyches, which had been intensely focused for so long on our business, my mother's illness, and keeping ourselves safe in the closet. Now we were able to let down our guard enough to take some creative initiative beyond our own shop.

We invited six literary-minded friends to a meeting and shared our vision of readers' theater. They agreed that it was an ideal participatory art form for community people who would enjoy creating productions and performing together without the burdens of memorizing scripts or putting in long hours of rehearsal. The Community Center was known locally for its high-quality theater productions, but most of the people who acted in the plays were either professionals or drama students. Our concept was designed to create opportunities for regular folks.

I suggested an Earth Day theme for the first presentation, which would be a collage of poetry and prose readings. I offered to put a script together with input and submissions of material from the readers. The group gave me the go-ahead, and we performed *Voices of the Earth* on the following Earth Day in mid-April. The same group of readers with some variations created and performed in subsequent years several more scripts that we generated together: *Women of Vision/Visions of Women; Georgia: A Literary Landscape;* and *The Wisdom of Foolishness: An Anthology of Literary Humor.* Eventually I wrote a play for the group called *Jack Grows a Beanstalk in the Quantum Field,* which turned out to be a milestone in my creative and spiritual life.

The readers' theater experience was important to Janice and me as a couple in that it gave us a shared means of involving ourselves in the community. And I believe the acceptance we enjoyed with readers' theater helped to build the confidence we needed to face other challenges that lay ahead.

In some ways these yearly theater events also helped to fill the creative void once filled by our gourd gatherings. We had not had gourds to harvest in January 1992, so we decided to stage a GAGG event on the following Fourth of July, which we called a Regourdda, i.e., Gourd Regatta.

Mildred Neville

A crowd watching the Regourdda

Wishing to make use of the lake at our new shop location, we decided to ask our friends to try their hands at making toy-sized gourd sailboats for the race.

The Regourdda was a success with 100 or more GAGG members attending, 15 of them bringing sailboat entries. A covered-dish picnic on the grassy lawn around the lake was followed by the viewing and judging of the boats—some of which were functional as well as funky—and then a race that started at the center of the pond. Whichever sailboat made it to the shore first would be the winner. There was almost no wind that evening, so the Regourdda itself wasn't much of a spectator sport. Finally someone's boat did make it to shore and was awarded the blue ribbon. As always with GAGG events, however, every entrant was a winner and received a certificate that solemnly declared:

> This is to certify that _____, having made a gourd
> boat with his/her own hands, did on this day honorably
> compete in the *Only Regourdda in the History of the World*
> and thus made a lasting contribution to gourd history and
> the celebration of creatively independent spirits every-
> where.

At the end of the evening everyone made wish-boats from small flat gourds. We had pre-drilled a hole in each so that people could place their secret wishes, written on tiny pieces of paper, inside the gourd and then place a candle in the hole, the kind of birthday candle that won't blow out. We took the wish-boats out into the lake, lit them, and set them afloat. The sight of 100 or so tiny flames floating on the pond was beautiful; some people stayed late and watched until they all burned out.

Barbara Williams with her regoudda entry

My own wish was as deceptively simple as the concept of a gourd boat: merely to stay afloat with my beloved partner and our awkwardly growing "child," Gourdcraft Originals and Company.

For the first couple of years after Leon Carter stopped growing gourds for us, Janice and I made arrangements with several local people who wanted to try farming for us on contract as he had done. When no one had much success, we began buying our gourds from a few large-scale growers located within 50 or 75 miles of us in the Cumming, Royston, and Athens areas. We still wanted our visitors to see gourd vines growing, so we always planted a few beside the arbor in front of our main entrance. We tended a garden-sized patch behind the building as well, but it rarely yielded many gourds for us, especially after the deer developed a taste for the vines.

Likewise, we weren't very successful growing wildflowers on the new property. After being disappointed initially to find only a few of our favorites already growing there, Janice, Patty, and I worked hard in the first years to establish additional species for our nature trail around the lake. We moved some plants from the previous shop location and our house: bloodroot, trout lily, columbine, black-eyed Susan. Few really took hold in their new settings, and many died out pretty quickly. We dug others that were plentiful along the roadsides: fire pink, butterfly weed, Queen Anne's lace, coreopsis, green-and-gold, smooth phlox, and more. The deer enjoyed some for snacks, and others apparently weren't happy in the spots we'd carefully chosen for them. I remember feeling bewildered and somewhat disgraced by our failure to succeed with the wildflower trail that had long been part of our dream.

And just as the plants themselves failed to thrive, so our wildflower T-shirt business began a gradual decline during the first year after the move. Competition among producers of nature-oriented tees was growing, and presumably the shops that had been carrying our shirts for several years were ready for a change. Within a year after our move, the shirt business was providing much less income than it had previously.

We saw a gradual increase in the number of visitors to our new location, but retail sales were not good enough to make up for shortfalls in the wholesale business. Moreover, we were learning from experience just how costly the property and buildings were to maintain. We worked hard to keep a positive attitude and tried new strategies to increase the flow of retail traffic, but we quickly began to feel financial stress.

In August 1992 a national magazine called *Country America* ran an article about our business. Though Janice and I had never heard of the publication before they contacted us for the interview and photo shoot, apparently their circulation was large. We received dozens of phone calls from all over the country in response to the article. Everyone wanted to know how they too could go into the gourd business.

For us the novelty soon wore off. We became irritated by the frequent calls, which seemed to come at the most inopportune times. If people had been asking for directions to our shop, we would have been more receptive. As it was, we had to grit our teeth and force ourselves to be polite to the callers, who seemed to think we had all day to instruct them in gourd growing and crafting.

One morning when I opened the shop and checked the answering machine for messages, I heard the gravelly voice of an elderly woman caller from Bakersfield, California. "I saw your article in *Country America*," the voice said, "and it brought back such memories of my childhood in Missouri. I wonder if I could order a gourd drinking dipper like the ones we used back on the farm." Her name was Flossie Phillips, and she brought me back, at least temporarily, from the busy, irritated person I was becoming to my old gourd girl self.

Flossie left her mailing address on the phone message in the hope that we would send her a catalog. Instead, I sent her a gourd dipper with a note saying that it was a gift from us. The gesture was a small random act of kindness that gave me a lift for a day. I didn't think much about it.

The six-page, handwritten letter I soon received from Flossie began:

> What a great surprise I got yesterday evening to receive the dipper gourd you sent me. Thank you a million times. I've wanted one for so many years. . . . I was born and raised in Missouri. And when I was young my parents never locked the doors. We had no meanness. Everyone was a neighbor to the others. I'm so thankful that I had loving parents and us kids were raised old-fashioned. And to be honest, and never tell a lie. Or steal anything. We were poor but didn't know it. For everybody was the same.

She was the proverbial salt of the earth. On typing paper hand-stamped with cardinals and roses, she went on to inform me that she had 11 pen pals "but none from Georgia." She also mentioned that she had collected 300 rubber stamps for decorating her stationary. Flossie won my heart. Her next letter, exuberantly stamped down the left side of each page with multicolored geese, bears, racoons, dogs, and squirrels, began, "Dear Pen Pal Number 12, Welcome!"

Flossie and I corresponded off and on for the next three years, enjoying a kind of anonymity and closeness at the same time. I had to say something in response to her soul-baring letters, so I did a little soul-baring of my own, often sharing my angst about the ups and downs of our business. Eventually I even came out to her in response to questions about whether I had a husband and kids, but I wondered if I'd hear from her again. Her next letter, stamped with palm trees, mushrooms, cattails, and clowns, was her usual fare except that at the end she simply said, "Tell your partner hello for me. I'll bet you both have lots of fun together. Write me."

Her letters, usually six or eight pages long, were full of the determination of a lonely person to stay busy and productive. In sending Flossie the dipper, I had opened the door to an outpouring of the Life Spark into my world. Her pages fairly vibrated with it, shouting a message of hope loud and clear. Sometimes I heard it, sometimes not. Predictably, I was the one who gradually let the correspondence drop, but Flossie had made a unique contribution to the gourd life.

gourd girls

Bob Rogers

Poster Lesbians

In March 1993, after she had been serving as an elder at Nacoochee Presbyterian Church for over a year, Janice learned quite by accident that self-affirming gay and lesbian people were not permitted to be ordained as deacons, elders, or ministers in the Presbyterian Church (U.S.A.). She was blind-sided; no one had told her about the "definitive guidance," as the national ban was called. Rev. John Hobbs, who may have been the only person at NPC who'd known of the policy at the time of her election, believed in Janice's right to serve. Moreover, he'd reasoned that because she was closeted she was not "self-affirming," in the language of the ban. Therefore he had chosen not to call attention to the policy.

Even after Janice and I told our parents the truth a year before, she had remained reluctant to come out more widely—and my wish to do so had continued to cause some friction between us. Yet now she was in the painful position of having to choose whether to remain closeted as a session member or to come out to that body. Her integrity left her no choice; she would affirm her identity as a lesbian. I was very proud but not at all surprised. Janice is the most honest person I have ever known.

She summoned her courage and told the group of 12 elders about our commitment to one another, explaining that she had realized upon learning of the ban that she was indeed self-affirming. She did not, she told them, see her love for me as morally wrong or something to be hidden. She resigned her office on the spot.

John Hobbs' leadership was instrumental in helping the group to articulate their response, but the appropriate sentiments came naturally to the individuals present. Surprised and unhappy to learn of the injustice represented by the "definitive guidance," they did not want to accept Janice's resignation. When she made it clear that she would no longer be attending meetings, they vowed to leave her position unfilled. Her empty seat would become a symbol and reminder of the brokenness of a national church that excluded gay and lesbian people from leadership positions.

Now when I look back on the meeting as Janice movingly described it to me that night, I remain amazed by the willingness of that group to face head-on an injustice about which most people were still in denial. Few church leaders were talking about gay and lesbian issues then—not even in the liberal "granola" church. It would have been all too easy to apologize to Janice, wiggle out of the conversation she was starting, and go on with business as usual. But these fine people would not take the easy way out, because the issue now had the face and name of a person they loved and respected.

The session decided to lead the church in a study of gay and lesbian issues over the next several years. Various Biblical scholars and theologians on both sides of the fence were invited to speak at Nacoochee about their interpretations of Scriptural references to homosexuality and their perspectives on the ordination question.

Janice—and I as her partner—became "poster lesbians," as we laughingly called ourselves, almost overnight. We took part in discussions and had the opportunity at long last to converse openly about our commitment to one another, about the experience of being closeted, about our certainty that there was nothing immoral about our love. We began to understand and articulate some of the subtle reasons for and manifestations of a prejudice with roots deep in our culture and in ourselves. It was an amazing time for us, bitter because it was occasioned by Janice's exclusion from leadership in the church but sweet because we were being heard and welcomed by most members of NPC.

A few people left the church as it became apparent that the vast majority of members favored inclusion. One found it necessary to voice her disgust directly to Janice. Not surprisingly, even some supportive people struggled to understand why our coming out was justified and necessary.

Bob Rogers

Nacoochee Presbyterian Church

One friend frequently compared her personal hardships with the plight of gays and lesbians, forgetting that, whatever her individual challenges, she enjoyed legal rights we could scarcely hope for in our lifetimes. Another made a special point of letting us know that he would be violently opposed if the two of us ever tried to marry in the church; still another demanded to be told why we wanted her to know about our sex life. We were deeply embarrassed but tried to explain that declaring ourselves as life partners was not about our sex life any more than her act of wearing a wedding band was about hers.

Our role as poster lesbians, consciously chosen but still difficult at times, required that we listen patiently to any comment or question directed to us and answer reasonably and respectfully. We had points to prove: that the stereotype of the angry, confrontational gay or lesbian person wasn't accurate; that we appreciated any thoughtful attempt at communication with us; that we were just ordinary people.

❧

The energy and attention Janice and I were devoting to the church controversy during 1993 and 1994 were a welcome diversion from our growing financial worries. Although in many ways we were still enthusiastic about our business, the stress of trying to make ends meet in the new location had taken away some of our youthful excitement. Imagining a prosperous future was no longer natural and effortless. The question of whether we had made a mistake in buying the new property hung in the air between us, largely unexplored. So long and hard had we believed in the importance of positive thinking that we were almost superstitious about admitting our doubts to each other.

At the beginning of 1994 we made the hard decision to sell our house in Blue Creek and move into the small cottage on the business property. The principle we owed on our line of credit was not terribly large by most people's standards, but we were uncomfortable with it and knew it would go higher during the lean winter months when few visitors would be coming to our shop. We had good equity in the house—enough to pay off our line of credit, make improvements to the cottage, and still have something left for a cushion. We reasoned that relieving our stress would make it worthwhile to give up the house.

Janice and I were both determined to be stoical about the decision. We reminded ourselves that we'd known all along the move might be necessary and that, in the scheme of things, we were lucky indeed to be in a position to rescue ourselves financially. Compared to most of the people in the world, we were still on easy street. Yet the house had marked an important milestone in our lives, and I think we should have let ourselves grieve more than we did.

As soon as we put our house on the market in January, we began moving the gourd workshop out of the cottage and into the basement of the main building so that we could renovate our new living space. I was unhappy about the necessity of working in the basement, but with a few minor improvements it has become a comfortable space as well as being convenient to the retail shop and pleasantly cool in summer. Reached by a long, narrow staircase, it is now known as "the gourd mines."

Interestingly, the cottage had the same floor plan as the downstairs of our house in Blue Creek, but in miniature. Our living space would shrink from about 1,700 to 750 square feet. With the help of our close friend and GAGG member Gloria Brown, who had helped us to design our dream house, we became engaged in the logistical challenge of figuring out how to make the cottage into a pleasant home. Another friend and GAGG member, Bill Morris—husband of June, who was still helping us in the shop at that time—did all of the carpentry, plumbing, and electrical work for a pittance. For weeks on end Janice and I spent most of our free time painting the dark paneling inside the cottage.

That March, when most of the work took place, happened to be a wet month. Perhaps because of the seemingly never-ending rain, we began to think of the compact little house as our ark, a refuge that would keep us high and dry as we escaped our financial demons. Like people living on a boat, we would make a game of living in a small, efficient space.

By the time we sold our house in July the cottage was ready. We settled in, relieved to have the ordeal of the sale and move behind us. Once again we lived in comforting proximity to Yonah and felt at home.

The experience of living in a tiny house proved enlightening for me. I quickly realized that life wasn't much different than before; in fact, the practicality, sensibility, and modesty of our new space were very appealing. Living in a small space forces a person to winnow down the supposed need for stuff, and I believe this process helped me to eliminate clutter on the inside. Some words from a sonnet by Gerard Manley Hopkins came back to me in those weeks of winnowing. The poet, struggling to understand hard times, asks the universal question: *Why?* and then answers it himself: *That my chaff might fly; my grain lie, sheer and clear.*

I took satisfaction in the knowledge that, even though our standard of living was still much higher than that of the average world citizen, the size of our new dwelling was more in line with world housing than our previous house had been. That knowledge felt good. My perspective on living space remains different from that of most people in our culture. Although admittedly I would enjoy a little more space, I would not want more than 1,000 square feet for the two of us even if we could afford a larger house. Janice isn't quite as radical as I am on the subject but does agree that small houses are an excellent idea.

Our financial bad luck continued. The water source for our cottage as well as the main building was a bored well only 45 feet deep, so we decided to use part of our profit from the sale of the house to drill a new well. We would have a safer water supply for ourselves and also satisfy a Health Department requirement for the future Gourd Time Café, a part of our dream we'd been unable to pursue because of our water source.

The well-drillers went down and down, and our bill went up and up—but no water was found. We gave up at 600 feet after spending $4,500 on a dry hole. The idea of continuing to gamble with what was left of our reserve seemed foolish. We were upset and frustrated about this loss, but we purchased a good water treatment system for our existing well and managed to put the disappointment behind us. Someday, we told ourselves, we'd try again.

For the remainder of that summer and into the fall Janice and I enjoyed a newfound freedom from worry. Having paid off our line of credit, we believed that the influx of cash would be the leg up that our business needed. We looked forward to rewarding ourselves for our sacrifice by taking a trip the following winter when our hours of operation would be shortened to two days a week.

In October we learned that Janice had a suspicious mass on her ovary. The only way to rule out a cancer diagnosis would be a hysterectomy. Like others have done, we went through frantic consultations with doctor after doctor, hastily made decisions and arrangements, living-in-fear for two or three weeks before her surgery was performed. Finally we heard the words we needed to hear: There was no cancer. I don't think I've ever experienced such a state of euphoria as I did in those first hours after learning the good news.

In the weeks after the surgery, as Janice recovered and the euphoric state wore off, I became very depressed about money. Our nest egg from the profit on the house would be almost gone by the time we paid high deductibles as well as our portion of medical bills. In addition to Janice's surgery, we had had medical bills for me—I had been diagnosed with Graves' disease earlier in the year and had required numerous doctors' visits and blood tests as well as expensive radioactive iodine treatments.

My illness, though it was eventually arrested, also contributed to my depression because it changed my physical appearance by causing swelling around my eyes and bulging of one eye. I was fortunate that the effects were not more severe, but paired with the rest of our circumstances and the stressfulness of the year, my bad feelings about my appearance were hard to cope with. I felt as though my face was a walking advertisement for how discouraged I felt inside. We had much to be thankful for in that we at least had the money to pay the medical bills, but at the time I could see only the futility of our efforts to get on our feet financially. We had cashed in our "ace in the hole," and we weren't much better off than before.

I struggled off and on with serious depression for the remainder of the 1990s but never made the decision to take medication. With Janice's love and patience and the blessing of continuing distractions from the Creative Force in my life, I got through the decade.

🐾

While our new little dwelling seemed like an ark in a physical sense, Nacoochee Presbyterian was similarly a refuge in an emotional sense. Our continuing involvement in the gay/lesbian study there was good for both of us. In November, after Janice's surgery in October, we participated in a panel discussion held at the church but also open to the public. Along with two panelists who were to speak against gay ordination, each of us was asked to tell our stories.

The event was important for us in that it was the first time we had come out in a public forum. Although we'd already been open with individuals and in group discussions, speaking our truth aloud in front of an audience made it official; our relationship would now be common knowledge. We feared that our struggling business would suffer, but we also believed that if gays and lesbians were to win equality in the church and beyond, everyone needed to do their small part to change hearts and minds.

I thought about the day when my high school Latin class read and acted out the story of Caesar leading his troops across the Rubicon River. There hadn't been enough speaking parts for everyone in my group, so I had volunteered to play the part of the river. As I lay giggling on the floor, Caesar stepped over me and made his famous pronouncement, "*Alea jacta est!*" or "The die is cast!" Our teacher had to explain to us what that meant, even in the English translation: There was no turning back for Caesar.

On the night when Janice and I spoke of our love for one another to a room full of people, I understood that Latin lesson in a new way. There would be no turning back for us now, no hiding in the closet, no chance of teaching school in White County again. Neither of us had any idea what we would do for a living if our business didn't survive.

Jim Reeves

The Thing With Feathers

ourdcraft Originals remained a creative stimulus as well as a source of anxiety. We had built a reputation on our ability to generate new ideas, and our feelings of obligation to customers kept us growing and changing even when we didn't feel inspired. This pressure to perform was probably my saving grace in that it kept me focused part of the time on the Creative Force instead of on business worries.

The idea of making calligraphy gourds was one rewarding result of my ongoing efforts to squeeze blood from the proverbial turnip-gourd. *Calligourdphy,* as we dubbed the concept, provided new artistic challenges and a means to enjoy some of my favorite lines of poetry. Now I was getting to be an English teacher on my own terms, selecting lines from Dickinson, cummings, Frost, Yeats, Hopkins, and Shakespeare to share with anyone persistent enough to read them in convoluted form on the gourds. And it was fun to make special gifts for friends and family members by carving their own favorite quotations or Bible verses.

On the first calligraphy gourd, still one of my favorites, I carved part of an Emily Dickinson poem:

> "Hope" is the thing with feathers—
> That perches in the soul—

Emory Jones

Calligourdphy gourds, left, *"Hope is the thing with feathers,"* right, *a gift I made for Janice with words from St. Exupery's* The Little Prince

And sings the tune without the words—
And never stops—at all—

For me, hope—or my sense of the Life Spark—literally did have feathers during some of our hardest times. No matter how down I was feeling, the sight of wild ducks on our pond never, never failed to bring me to life and send me scurrying for binoculars and bird book. One fall in particular we were blessed with visits from numerous species: mallards, wood ducks, ringnecks, buffleheads, blue-winged teals, and even mergansers.

For a period of a week or so the ringnecks came every day. Some days there were six or seven, other days, just one or two. Floating effortlessly and soundlessly on the pond, they were a stunning black-and-white picture of the serenity I coveted. Several times a day I slipped down to the pond and tried to get close to them. Unruffled by my approach but very much aloof, they always floated quickly to the other side, but as though not wanting to desert me, did not fly away.

The wood ducks, the most dramatically beautiful of all the ducks that visited, were also the most elusive. I wrote about them in a newspaper column:

> At dusk I hear the soft squeaky voices of the wood ducks and see their faint outlines as they hunt acorns in the little grove of burr oaks near the pond. I want to come closer, but they have taught me that I must respect their wildness. The ducks often have to share the grove with a yearling deer, but they get along well together; they share their wildness, while I am only a would-be intruder.
>
> We humans sometimes think we own the planet. But as I watch the ducks in the near-darkness, it seems to me that we're the strangers here. We're not privy to all that goes on in the world; we are outsiders, and we are outclassed.

I now see that my fascination with wildlife not only took me out of myself, but also put my worries in perspective against the backdrop of the natural world. Even the regular comings and goings of Canada geese, considered pests by some people, always gave me a lift. One pair nested yearly in the same spot beside the pond, despite the fact that predators invariably destroyed their nests or their babies if they hatched. Like the geese themselves, we hoped every year would be the year that their luck changed. And perhaps we took a lesson in perseverance from them.

The most comforting sight of all was a great

Priscilla Wilson

Our own gourdegret!

Thanksgiving scene

blue heron that visited regularly. Amazingly, it appeared when I most needed to see it; so perfect was its timing that I became almost superstitious about this magical bird's way of keeping its hand on my spiritual pulse. The same heron, or perhaps another one, still graces us with its presence from time to time.

🍂

The same feelings of obligation to the public that kept us developing new items to sell, such as calligraphy gourds, also kept us working on ideas that paid only in laughter, such as the silly fixtures we made for our guest restroom. The gourd toilet tissue holder, paper towel holder, and pulls on cabinet doors continue to make people smile, as does our gourd cash register at the checkout counter.

We also kept up our tradition of creating funny characters and placing them near the highway for passers-by to enjoy. During the mid-1990s the

American Gothic, *gourd-style*

Janice Lymburner

scenes became more elaborate: a game of catch with a gourd ball suspended on a fishing line between two players; a William Tell scene featuring a bow and arrow made from gourds, along with the apple on the little boy's head; a suffragette urging people to vote on Election Day; and dozens more. Some of my personal favorites were the Pilgrim shooting a gourd turkey with a gourd musket and our own version of the famous Grant Wood painting *American Gothic*.

Neighbors rewarded us by honking when they passed or coming inside to thank us for our efforts. Eventually, after several thefts, we had to begin placing the scenes in front of our main building, farther away from the road so they'd be less accessible to pranksters. Still, the bursts of creative energy that resulted in the scenes were life-giving for Janice, Patty, and me.

Art is often defined as a form of communication, a two-way street in which the audience plays a role just as essential as that of the artist. Philosophers can debate *ad infinitum* the question of whether art does or does not exist without the observer, but I know that the people who enjoyed our place in the mid- and late 1990s kept me going.

On good days I felt suspended, cradled between the Creative Force on one side and the responsiveness of my fellow humans on the other. Each time I heard laughter overhead as I worked in the basement, each time passers-by honked their horns in approval of our scenes, the flagging Life Spark in me was fanned. It was uncanny how many visitors wrote in our guest book just what we needed to hear, words such as "There's a sweet spirit here" or "Keep on gourding" or "Your place is a blessing to all that come in." One fine soul wrote:

> It is beautiful to be walking upon the road of life and to happen across such lovely people. Keep sharing your love and passion with the passers-by and inspire others to walk with you in harmony.

A Two-Church Family

As our involvement with Nacoochee Presbyterian Church deepened, so did our friendship with Rev. John Hobbs. Janice and I were moved by his sensitivity to the plight of gays and lesbians in society and the church. In fact, his interest in the subject seemed to go far beyond what one would expect—even of a compassionate minister taking a progressive stance on social justice issues. We began to wonder about his own sexual orientation.

As I have said, John was married and had two children, who were by this time in their late teens. Janice and I were fearful for the whole family but told ourselves that our suspicions were wrong, that we shouldn't be speculating. Meanwhile, we saw more and more of John. He often dropped by the gourd shop, presumably to lend us emotional support. But gradually he began to allow us to see how deeply troubled he himself was. Finally in the summer of 1995 John came out to us as a gay man. Our hearts broke for him and for his wife, Esther.

Like so many gay and lesbian people who marry, John had suppressed the knowledge of his orientation and had believed that his faith in God, his love for Esther and their children, and his focus on the needs of his parishioners would make it possible for him to have a good and useful life without facing the nagging questions inside himself. Now, with the

John Hobbs with Janice left *and Priscilla*

growing controversy in the Presbyterian Church (U.S.A.) as a catalyst and with Janice and me as well as other friends providing support, he finally let go of his secret.

In the difficult months that followed it seemed as though John was always at our house. We often told him jokingly that he was giving us the gift of an excuse to avoid our own problems. It was true. We functioned and kept our business going, but our emotional energies were with John and the church. Gradually he came out to the church community and faced an uncertain future. Esther, blind-sided and devastated by her husband's revelation, eventually filed for divorce. Congregation members grieved for John, Esther, and the children—and for their own loss, individually and corporately, of this family so dear to them.

In the summer of 1996 John moved to Chicago and took a job as director of the Interfaith Council for the Homeless. Esther and the children, both of whom were now in college, moved back to her home state of Virginia, where she took a job in her field of social work. Janice and I remain friends with all of them and are thankful that both Esther and John have found happiness with new life partners. Their lives are much different—and better—than anyone could have foreseen during that painful period in their lives. John, still denied a pastorate in the Presbyterian Church (U.S.A.), eventually became affiliated with the United Church of Christ, the only Christian denomination whose pulpits are open to gay and lesbian persons. In the spring of 2005 he received a call to serve a church in Chicago.

❧

Nacoochee Church had re-elected Janice to the session at the beginning of 1996, this time doing so in open defiance of the church's ban against leadership by gays and lesbians in ordained positions. As both a session member and a close friend of John Hobbs, Janice found herself at the center of the upheaval in the church. She was completely immersed in the church's pain and the struggle to hold the congregation together, first during John's coming out and departure and then during the 18-month transition period while the search committee did its work of finding a new pastor.

I began feeling predictably jealous of Janice's relationship with the church and the amount of time she spent there. Feeling a need to make a

Sunday school at NPC with Dillon Nelson, Rebecca Steele, and Janice

difference in my own way, I became active in the Georgia Equality Project (GEP), a statewide political advocacy group for gays and lesbians. This Atlanta-based group was in need of representation from rural areas, and I agreed to serve on the Board of Directors. For a couple of years I went to Atlanta regularly for meetings and lobbying sessions at the state capitol. Janice encouraged me in these endeavors and attended a few of the GEP activities with me. In four or five years we had moved together from the closet to church activism to activism within the political system.

Meanwhile I was coming to the realization that I couldn't limit myself theologically to the Christianity of my childhood. Had I not stayed away from the church for 15 years while Janice and I were closeted, my beliefs might have remained more or less unchallenged, but distancing myself for so long changed my perspective. When I'd returned to church with Janice, it was almost as though I was coming from another planet and was seeing my former religion through different eyes.

I tried to wipe my mental slate clean and take a fresh look at the concept of God, or the Life Spark, as I had come to think of it. When I asked myself where this spark or life impulse might manifest itself at the most basic level, I saw the whirling electrons inside atoms. My knowledge of physics was as limited as a 10-year-old's; I had not even taken high school physics, so great had been my homophobic desire to appear feminine, i.e., disinterested in science.

Now I found an elementary book about atoms, and the new frontier of quantum physics began to open up to me. I wasn't the only person searching for God in the sub-atomic world: world-renowned scientists such as David Bohm and Fritjof Capra had found spiritual truths there and written at length about their insights. These two in particular helped me to see that, though quantum physics cannot explain the existence of the Life Spark, it can illuminate the workings and principles of this force in amazing ways.

As my explorations took me far afield from traditional Christian theology, I was more and more uncomfortable with the fact that my life, along with Janice's, had come to revolve around Nacoochee Presbyterian Church. Of course I had a choice about whether to continue attending services, and yet the thought of pulling away from this loving group of people was difficult. They had held us in their very hearts, welcomed and supported us as we stumbled out of the closet, and breathed life back into the suffocated parts of our spirits.

I tried to explain my religious differences to a few close church friends, but they didn't understand why I was letting theology come between the church community and me. "There are plenty of people at church who are questioning like you," they said. "So what? Nobody expects you to believe a certain way." That was true, but my discomfort was about my own integrity and about the fact that taking part in traditional church services was making it harder for me to reimagine God in my own way.

Religious differences have always created challenges for life partners, and Janice and I were no exception. We discussed theology and my un- happiness at Nacoochee endlessly in an effort to come to terms with one another. We argued, sobbed, sympathized, and argued some more, sometimes late into the night. Janice understood my views far better than anyone and agreed with many of them, but she still considered herself a Christian and remained focused on her responsibility to help bring about change in the institutional church. She had a powerful dream during this period that strengthened her resolve, a dream in which Jesus told her how important her efforts were for gays and lesbians in the church.

In her view, she needed my help to carry out her mission; she needed me to be present with her at Nacoochee so that we would be reminders that stable gay and lesbian couples exist. I understood, wanted to help, and most of all didn't want to hurt Janice. But each time I had to decide whether to attend a church service, I was choosing between Janice and the cause on one hand and my own religious search on the other.

For several years I chose Janice and the cause over myself. Each time I thought I was ready to make a change, something happened to keep me at church. During much of 1995 and 1996, that something had been my desire to support John Hobbs. As the time for his departure approached, I told myself I would begin pulling away. Then in 1996, not long before John left Nacoochee, the General Assembly of the Presbyterian Church (U.S.A.) passed an amendment to the *Book of Order,* known as Amend- ment B, which was intended to codify the ban in a more permanent way than the "definitive guidance" had done; in other words, its passage would mandate that gays and lesbians continue to be blocked from serving as pastors, elders, and deacons. Each presbytery or regional church body throughout the country had to vote on ratification of this amendment.

In 1997 discussions were held at the first two quarterly meetings of Northeast Georgia Presbytery in preparation for the vote. Although there were within this largely conservative group a handful of advocates for gays and lesbians who spoke and worked tirelessly to defeat the amendment, Janice was the only openly lesbian elder who was willing to speak publicly. She did not enjoy the limelight, but she bore the responsibility of giving the issue a face and speaking aloud on behalf of those whose voices were silenced by fear.

During both meetings in which the amendment was debated, Janice spoke against it before the body of several hundred people with a quiet dignity, strength, and radiance that were beautiful to behold. Interested persons who were not commissioners were welcome to attend presbytery meetings, and I always attended along with other supporters from NPC. I was exceedingly proud of Janice at these times; I believe everyone present, regardless of their views, was in awe of her grace and courage. Nevertheless, Northeast Georgia Presbytery did approve the amendment, as did the majority of presbyteries in the denomination.

Some gays and lesbians left the denomination in protest. Though angry and hurt, Janice was invested in the idea of continuing to work for change within the church. She not only stayed, but she served a second consecutive term on the session before rotating off as required by church polity.

Janice also taught Sunday school for several years during and after the nationwide debates over Amendment B. I remember well how important this role was to her, how much time she spent preparing lessons and visual aids, and how deeply she cared about her pupils. It was clear to me that teaching was life-giving for Janice, a new way of channeling her energies after the defeat.

Janice's sexual orientation was a non-issue with parents at NPC; in fact, one parent said she felt especially comfortable having Janice as her child's teacher because Janice understood God to be loving and compassionate rather than vengeful and angry. Other parents credited her with their children's eagerness to come to church and to stay involved as they grew older.

One former pupil, now 19, told me she had learned more about the Bible in Janice's class than in all the years of her religious education combined. She remembers Janice's way of explaining Scripture lessons so the children could understand them, and she explains that now when she takes part in theological discussions as a young adult she can articulate and trust her own beliefs largely because of Janice's influence. "And," she adds, "back then I didn't know she was a lesbian—not that it mattered!"

☙

Soon after the passage of Amendment B, I began visiting the newly formed Georgia Mountains Unitarian Universalist Church (GMUUC) in Dahlonega, 25 miles from Sautee. The UU religion does not subscribe to any one set of theological beliefs but honors all faith traditions. Instead of one religious creed, UUs agree upon seven principles, e.g., *the inherent worth and dignity of every human being* and a *free and responsible search for truth and meaning*. These principles provide a framework within which every person may believe as she is led while enjoying the fellowship and support of a church community. Congregations within the Unitarian Universalist Association are inclusive of gays and lesbians in hiring and in election of leaders.

I knew only one person at GMUUC when I first began visiting but was welcomed warmly and soon felt comfortable worshiping with my new free-thinking friends. The services were much different from traditional Protestant services, with readings drawn from a wealth of sources including the Torah, the Koran, and the Bhagavad-Gita as well as the Bible and various literary works. Silent meditation was the norm instead of supplicatory prayer, and the hymns employed broad, inclusive language amazingly applicable to anyone's beliefs.

Gradually I began attending the UU church more and Nacoochee Presbyterian less. The transition period was difficult, especially for Janice, but she respected the fact that I was finally being true to myself. What saddened both of us most was that we wanted to attend church together. But we soon realized that, if each of us attended with the other once a month, we would be in church together two Sundays out of four. We made a conscious decision to put a positive face on our new identity as a two-church family.

Now Janice and I see that together we've contributed to and benefited from both churches. Nacoochee will always be the home of our hearts, but the UU church has helped us both come to a place of embracing all religions, including Christianity. Now I can embrace Christianity as well as Buddhism, Taoism, and quantum physics. One doesn't have to understand or agree with every tenet of every faith to celebrate the human impulse to worship and to strive for betterment.

Sailing as Metaphor

The late 1990s found Gourdcraft Originals still barely holding its own. Looking back, I think our disillusionment was probably as difficult to deal with as the actual financial stress. We had believed in the myths that "if you build a better mousetrap, the world will beat a path to your door" and that hard work is always rewarded—but our experience was proving these ideas untrue. We had worked very hard and created a unique destination where people could have fun, learn something, enjoy our grounds, and buy quality handmade items unavailable anywhere else. Yet the business wisdom that prevailed was "location, location, location." We were off the beaten track. Despite our efforts to promote ourselves, visitors didn't appear at our door in droves hungering to buy gourd art.

Of course countless American dreamers have experienced painful wake-up calls as we did. Janice and I have watched businesses in bad locations come and go over the years and have felt much compassion for those entrepreneurs who, often in a matter of months, had to give up on their dreams. We've laughingly said many times that the only difference between those people who account for the high percentage of business failures and us is that we're willing to accept a lower standard of living than they are.

Considering that we were determined to buck the conventional wisdom about location, we did attract a fair number of people, partly thanks to continued free publicity from occasional newspaper, magazine, or television coverage. A couple of features in *Southern Living* magazine brought in numerous visitors, as did the Home and Garden Network's program "A Gardener's Diary." Once here, most guests greatly enjoyed our place and made purchases, even if only raw gourds for do-it-yourself projects.

We always speculated that a higher percentage of people spent money with us than visitors to the average shop, but we needed far greater numbers than we were getting. Our overhead was out of proportion to our income. In addition to the mortgage payments, the maintenance of our property and buildings was eating up every dollar we made.

Janice and I both entertained our most serious doubts yet about staying in business. We were tired of having our sense of well-being so closely tied to the ups and downs of shop sales and maintenance crises. Always facing a long laundry list of major repairs and weighing which one was needed most desperately, we imagined how freeing it might be to sell the property and find jobs.

Each of us had times when we were ready to let go. "Just say the word," Janice would say to me—or vice versa—"and we'll give it up." But we were never ready at the same time. We discussed too the fact that one of us should feel free to get a "real job" and allow the other to continue with the business. Yet neither made a move. Janice might have gone back to the classroom, but she was no longer employable as a teacher because of her sexual orientation. I didn't know what I wanted to do. I searched my soul and consciousness, meditated, prayed, read about how to find my *dharma*.

The only thing I felt drawn to do was join the Peace Corps, and Janice was open to exploring that possibility. But we quickly learned that, because only married couples were given shared assignments, the two of us could not serve together. Even though the Peace Corps proudly claimed not to discriminate on the basis of sexual orientation, in reality they did so indirectly on the basis of marital status.

So we limped along, our spirits held up by our church involvements, families, and friends. Daddy and Berenice still lived three miles away on the property adjoining our former house, and we saw them often. Daddy treated us to dinner at restaurants we couldn't have afforded, and Berenice often shared her wonderful talents for cooking—and telling jokes—with us. We were open with them about our discouragement and money worries but didn't disclose fully the depth of our despair or the strain it was placing on our relationship. They sympathized, encouraged us by their belief in what we were doing, and brought a steady stream of their houseguests from Beaufort and Savannah to see the shop and buy our work.

Janice's mother and her now-husband Don Webb were very supportive as well. The two of them came up from Atlanta often for visits and genuinely shared in our excitement about whatever new idea we were pursuing at the time. When we gave a party, they were here to help, and Don always wanted to help us with maintenance or yard projects as well. They too were concerned and sympathetic about our financial stress but never doubted our ability to survive and never encouraged us to give up.

Come to think of it, I don't remember any family member or friend ever suggesting that we give up. We had a circle of close friends with whom we spent many social evenings, and they were also aware of our struggle; but everyone seemed to take it for granted that we would stay in business. Even when we occasionally mentioned that we were looking into other options such as the Peace Corps, no one seemed to take us seriously. Whether consciously or unconsciously, our loved ones seemed to use denial as well as laughter to help us escape our cloud of worry for hours at a time.

Meanwhile, like a child's inflatable clown that can't be knocked down, the Creative Force popped up again and again with some new impulse or another. I was often afraid to get excited during that period of malaise, afraid Janice would be hurt if new efforts didn't work out. But she would grin at me and say, "Aw, c'mon, let's get excited!" And we would.

In the winter of 1998 we decided to open two rooms for bed-and-breakfast lodgers the following spring. We consolidated our retail space in the main building to free up two bedrooms with private baths, and then set about furnishing and decorating the rooms. It was fun making gourd accessories for them: lamps, wastebaskets, ice buckets, even night lights with pierced designs for the bathrooms. These soon became popular items in our shop, as did the gourd lamp bases with traditional shades.

We changed the sign at our entrance to read *The Gourd Place*, which sounded more inclusive of a bed-and-breakfast than *Gourdcraft Originals*. The B&B was fun and brought in enough revenue to repay our investment. Within a couple of years, however, drought conditions prevailed in northeast Georgia, and the water level in our well dropped quite low. We decided not to take lodgers until conditions improved. By the time the drought ended about three years later, we were involved with other projects and never reopened the lodging rooms. The most important purpose served by the short B&B chapter was that of giving Janice and me new energy and hope during a long winter.

The spring that our B&B opened we made a game of gourd croquet, or "goofy gourds," and set it up in the yard for guests to play. The mallets came from a regular set, but the wickets were curved dipper gourds and the balls, round ones about the size of a grapefruit. People loved seeing the game set up in the backyard, although we and our friends were the only people who actually played. Needless to say, the balls didn't hold up well!

Another new creation in 1998 was a line of gourd-character note cards that we called *Gword-Play*. I created these on the computer using clip-art cartoon people and giving them gourds as heads. The cards included Little Gourdy Two-Shoes, Ed-gourd Allen Poe, Gourdilocks and the Three Bears, and a dozen more. They were not particularly profitable but did provide me with a new outlet; I worked on the computer obsessively for hours at a time to put them together. Our visitors rewarded me with their laughing enjoyment of the cards.

We also began designing gourd T-shirts that took the place of our wildflower shirts and carried messages: *Celebrate Diversity. It's a Gourd Thing* was the first, and then came *Simplify. It's Gourd for the Earth; The Gourd Old Days;* and *Let the Gourd Times Roll.* The creation of the first gourd shirts led to a new way of using our business as a platform to share beliefs and values. Friends and customers let us know that our messages resonated with them. These were times when we understood that money couldn't buy the unique fun and satisfaction our business gave us.

❦

Perhaps it was our continuing struggle to stay afloat that made me want to try making gourd sailboats again. The effort provided me with yet another chance to learn a lesson that has become the story of my working life, maybe everyone's: *Good things don't come easy.* In my case, *gourd things don't come easy.*

I only wanted to make a few simple boats to anchor on our pond for the enjoyment of visitors. How hard could that be? I'd forgotten what little I had learned when trying to make boats for the Regourdda six years earlier. Having carefully selected four gourds with flat bottoms, I tested them to see how they would ride in the water and coated them with marine varnish. Then I sewed beautiful sails of red, blue, yellow, and green nylon and placed them on dowel masts that I mounted on the uncut gourds in various ways. These boats, to my mind simple and elegant, had no keels cluttering their design. The keel, as I later learned, is the under-water part of a boat that stabilizes it.

One bright spring Sunday morning after Janice left for church, I took my toys out in our little rowboat and placed them on the shining water. There was no wind, but the boats looked beautiful floating there. I sat still in the rowboat for a few minutes enjoying the morning sun, the sparkles on the water, and the sight of my little fleet.

Finally I paddled back to shore and went inside for the camera. By the time I got back to the edge of the pond the wind had picked up a little and one boat had capsized. I didn't let it bother me; one out of four wasn't bad. I took several pictures, and then a gust of wind took another boat, and another, and another. Hurriedly I paddled back out to rescue all the boats before customers arrived and saw what a ridiculous failure I was.

In the next months I worked off and on at trying to make boats that wouldn't embarrass me. As with the raft-building fiasco 10 years before, my few short-lived successes made me want to keep trying. I developed a backache that seemed permanent as I pushed and pulled the rowboat in and out of the lake in order to test and then rescue capsized sailboats.

Sometimes beauty must be found in function rather than simplicity of design. I accepted the necessity of putting keels on the boats, and my success curve went way up. Ultimately I developed a method of making gourd catamarans using two club-shaped gourds held in parallel position by clamps and a wooden framework. The mast and the keel as well as the anchor line are attached to this framework. Although the boats are always in need of maintenance, they rarely turn over nowadays. It's always thrilling to see them stand on their sides in strong winds and then right themselves.

It is hard, even for me, to understand how making toy sailboats can be so meaningful to a woman over 50. In truth, it is the sailing of them that is more meaningful—yet that is so only because of my struggle to make them. The boats have become a metaphor for my efforts to get it right, to find a way to stay afloat, and more, to work with the winds that come my way.

For several years now Janice and I have enjoyed a tradition of launch-

Gourd sailboats staying afloat

ing new or refurbished sailboats on Easter Day. If we're lucky, one of them survives until the end of the December holiday season, when we put them in dry dock. Many visitors to The Gourd Place seem to be charmed by the boats and to appreciate the fact that they cannot be seen anywhere else in the world. Some want to buy them, but they are not for sale. We try to encourage people to make their own and thus take a rewarding—and frustrating—spiritual journey of their own.

I've often thought wonderingly about the difficult day during my mother's illness, long before gourd sailboats crossed my mind, when "Smooth Sailing" became my comforting internal theme song and uncanny forecaster of the future.

gourd girls

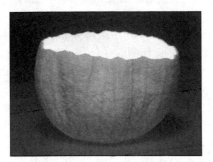

Playing With Fire

*B*y the beginning of 1999 I was ready to make a change. As our late friend John Head would have said, "Sometimes you gotta go ahead and do *something*, even if it's *wrong*." I was not ready to give up on our business altogether, but I thought a part-time job might relieve some financial stress and allow me to test myself outside of the gourd world.

I began putting the word out that I was looking for a "real job." Soon a friend told me about a part-time Rural Services Coordinator position at Rape Response, a rape crisis center based in nearby Gainesville. I went for an interview and hit it off instantly with the director, Terri Strayhorn. Unwilling to be closeted in the job, I came out to Terri right away and was glad to learn that my sexual orientation was not an issue for her or the Board of Rape Response.

The job offered flexible hours, depending on the schedule of meetings I needed to attend. I usually worked three or four days a week at The Gourd Place and two or three for Rape Response. The job took me out of my own head and into the worlds of nonprofit organizations, health care, law enforcement, and most important, victims of crime. Although the information I learned was hard to live with, its impact was mitigated by the upbeat, positive attitudes of my co-workers. They managed to stay focused, not on the horrors of sexual assault, but on the healing process for victims and on prevention education programs that they offered in the public schools.

Our new arrangement was difficult for Janice at first, but she rose to the challenge, operating the business without me. She knew that each of us had to find our own ways to fight the malaise that gripped us and stir the waters in hopes that new life would surface.

I worked for Rape Response for a little over three years. The experience was affirming for me in that, after being out of the work force for 23 years at that point, I saw that I could actually get a job and function in it. Receiving a check every two weeks was a novel and uplifting experience for one who, after being self-employed for so long, had come to see paychecks as an unfortunate necessity rather than a pleasant reward.

On a late September Saturday evening in 1999 Janice and I celebrated the silver anniversary of our life partnership with a big outdoor pot-luck by the lake. We were blessed with beautiful weather, a full moon, and more than 100 people in attendance, including our parents, our sisters, and my niece. We'd requested that there be no gifts, but the group presented us with a silver gourd piggy bank containing a gift of cash that paid for the party expenses many times over.

Each of us said a few words of thanks to the group, and Janice included in her remarks the secret, in her opinion, to our success as a couple. She explained that the Bluebird Wish, part of the Camp Fire Girl teachings for the youngest children in the program, was something the two of us had shared at Camp Toccoa, where we'd met:

> The Bluebird Wish:
> To have fun
> To learn to make beautiful things
> To remember to finish what I begin
> To want to keep my temper most of the time
> To go to interesting places
> To learn about trees, flowers, and birds
> And make friends.

I had made silver sails for two of our gourd boats and placed them on the lake just before the party as a surprise for Janice. We were still sailing

Family members at our anniversary party, left to right: *Bill Wilson, Berenice Wilson, Janice, Nancy Lymburner, Priscilla, Janice's sister Sandy Shapiro, Priscilla's sister Nancy Nutt, and Priscilla's niece Priscilla Nutt Muir*

together after 25 years. *"Sail on, silver girl,"* the universe seemed to be saying that night in the words of Paul Simon. *"Your time has come to shine . . . all your dreams are on their way."* We were still wondering whether we were on a ship that would take us down; but we were sailing together, and we were among friends. For months we felt buoyed by the outpouring of friendship we received that night.

❧

One of the strangest and most powerful gifts of my career came to me in the early days of 2000. I will always believe the gift—or my ability to recognize it—was owing in part to the peace and satisfaction I had derived from both the 25th anniversary party and the Rape Response job.

I was driving alone on Georgia Highway 365 and thinking of nothing in particular when a picture came into my mind: an image of a dried, broken gourd in the field. I saw clay inside this shard as though a heavy rain had caused it to wash into the gourd. During our farming days Janice and I had often observed slabs of clay sticking to the outside of dried gourds in the field at harvest time. I had wondered whether early potters might have been inspired by such natural formations. But the image that dropped into my head on that January day showed me a different possibility. "*Oh*," I said to myself, "maybe the clay goes on the *inside* of the gourd instead of the *outside*."

The picture shifted to liquid clay being poured into a gourd mold. It was clear to me that the images I was seeing represented a way to make ceramic objects carrying the imprint of the textures and veins on the inside of the gourds; yet the concept seemed far-fetched and somehow eerie. "What a weird idea," I said aloud to myself in the car. I'd never had the least desire to work with clay. My interest in the origins of pottery had existed only because of the role gourds might have played in inspiring early potters.

The images I saw that day—and the word *slip*, which had accompanied the pictures even though it wasn't in my limited vocabulary of pottery terms—haunted me. Beautiful and varied textures of thousands of gourd interiors that I had seen in 20-odd years passed through my mind. I described the concept to Janice, who, like me, didn't know whether to take it seriously or not. The two of us had often talked of our hopes for a brand-new idea that would revive our flagging dream and help us financially. Could this be the idea we'd been wishing for? We both recalled with wonder the day 21 years earlier when the gourd globe idea had excited us so much that we'd considered renaming our business *Gourd Earth Products*. Now the phrase carried new meaning; perhaps we would begin making products from gourds and earth in collaboration with one another.

I began talking with a few friends about the gourd pottery idea and confirmed my hunch that *slip* was indeed a word for liquid clay. Bob Owens, a Foothills Guild founding member and much-admired potter, explained to me that the process I was contemplating, normally accomplished using plaster molds, was called slip-casting. Bob and I both saw the idea of my making gourd pottery as weird and laughable; we joked about the notion that I might compete with him someday. Yet he was genuinely hopeful that the idea might work and encouraged me to buy a gallon of stoneware slip, which I did.

For the next few months I was alternately in heaven and hell as I worked obsessively to make my unusual vision a reality. Of the first 8 or 10 experiments, only one tiny pot about two inches in diameter and half an inch deep came out of its gourd mold without cracking, but that beautifully veined little pot kept me going. I tried different kinds of slip, different ways of treating the inside surface of the gourds to help the clay release without cracking, and different casting times. Eventually I had a couple of respectable-sized pieces of pottery to show for my efforts, and Bob fired them for me. The two of us shared a thrilling moment when we held those first gourd bowls still warm from the kiln.

Janice and I told our friend Betsy Stoinoff, an acclaimed clay and metal sculptor from Hiawassee, about my experiments. We had known Betsy since 1977 when we exhibited together in the Georgia Mountain Fair. Having made molds and used the slip-casting process in her work, she was captivated by the idea, but she eventually convinced me that if I really wanted to produce gourd pottery I would have to make traditional molds using my successful gourd castings as models. I began learning the difficult art of making plaster molds, suffering "plaster disasters," as I called them, almost daily. Patiently and tirelessly Betsy coached me in mold-making during many late-night telephone sessions.

I was still in my Rape Response job, so time for doing much-needed gourd production work was limited. We were always short of standard items such as containers, planters, toys, and Christmas ornaments to sell in the shop, and so I had to squeeze in time for working on the gourd pottery project without knowing if my efforts would ever pay off. Janice encouraged me in spite of the fact that financial rewards seemed unlikely. She could see that whatever else the new project was, it was life-giving for me.

Now as I think of that period I remember that my metabolism was in high gear; that I drove Janice and our families and friends crazy with my constant, manic talk about pottery; that I was exhausted all the time; that I was thankfully conscious of how alive I felt. "Once you get that clay under your fingernails," a grinning Bob Owens had told me, "you're hooked forever."

Janice and I soon bought a used kiln and learned to fire it with continued coaching from Bob, Betsy, and others. As I gained a little confidence I began to disregard some of their advice, taking risks with firing that many clay artists wouldn't have taken. "Girl, you're playing with fire," Betsy once said to me when I told her about my unorthodox methods. Yet I think she saw my growing insistence on following my own instincts as a sign that I was becoming a real clay artist.

The transformation that takes place in the firing of clay is magic, and for me personally the process was magic as well. The gourd pottery concept transformed *me* from the permanently discouraged person I had become to a person who felt reconnected to the Life Spark. I was indeed playing with fire.

By late summer we were producing enough gourd pottery to start thinking about giving Gourd Impressions its debut in our retail shop. The success rate for original gourd castings had improved, and I had made plaster molds with which I could cast 8 or 10 different bowls and small vases. In lieu of a party for my 50th birthday in September we held a pottery open house. As it happened, the actual date of the event fell on my late mother's birthday in October. I felt very close to Mama, the person who'd influenced my creative life more than anyone, and longed to show her the gourd pottery.

Attendance and sales at the open house were good, and many people shared our excitement over the birth of Gourd Impressions. An ancient connection between the earth and one of its plant products had been brought into tangible form, a form that would allow people to use gourds in daily life as our ancestors had done.

Meanwhile Janice and I wondered if we should try to patent the new

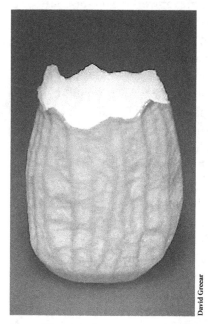

David Greear

Gourd luminary

process. We talked with a patent agent and an attorney about our prospects and the cost of applying for legal protection. Each believed we had a reasonable chance of getting the patent but estimated that the price could be $5,000– $7,000—out of our reach. We then learned that Donald Studley, a slight acquaintance of ours from Cleveland, was a retired patent attorney. His wife was the niece of Ruth Stovall Head, our former gardening mentor from the old days of growing gourds on the Stovall farm, so we had a pleasant connection with Mr. Studley. He generously offered to help us apply for the patent and assured us that his fees would be affordable.

David Greear

Gourd Impressions pottery

As it turned out, Donald Studley never accepted payment for the crucial help he gave us. He guided us through the first part of the application process and then became ill with lung cancer. He was unable to continue the work but convinced me that I was capable of finishing the job myself. Our application was filed at the end of April 2001, a month after Mr. Studley's death. Whether the patent ever issues or not, we will always be grateful to this kind man.

The patent process has proven convoluted and frustrating, requiring a long series of amendments and formal written arguments back and forth between the patent examiner and me. Several times I have sought advice from Kenneth Watkins, the patent agent we had consulted in the beginning. He believes in our product and has generously advised us *pro bono*. As this book goes to press the outlook is still good, but we do not yet have the patent in hand.

Throughout 2001 and 2002 I continued to pour much effort into the pottery. Janice became very much involved in its production as well, glazing while she minded the shop and sharing in decisions about new forms and glazes. We were two old dogs happily learning new tricks and enjoying an infusion of energy into ourselves and our business. Gourd Impressions appealed to people who had never been drawn to the gourds, and we saw an influx of newcomers to the shop.

By the spring of 2002 I had phased out my Rape Response job and was once again working full time and more on both gourds and pottery. Patty Workman had added pottery-making skills to her large repertoire, and her enthusiastic help was making it possible for us to offer a complete line of tableware as well as dozens of vases and vessels in several different glazes.

Although our money worries had not evaporated completely, pottery sales were giving us more peace of mind than we had experienced in a long time. Like gourdcrafting, however, pottery production proved to be too labor-intensive to help us in any dramatic way as long as we remained small. I am resistant to the idea of managing a pottery factory just as I was years ago to the notion of a gourd factory. Janice and I are hopeful that we might be able to sell or license the invention to a pottery manufacturer instead of mass-producing it ourselves.

I've joked before that gourds are the Rodney Dangerfield of art forms: they get no respect. My experience of becoming a clay artist has confirmed the truth of that statement. The difference we observe in people's attitudes about our pottery compared with our gourd work is striking. I've noticed that artist friends who tour the basement workshop now refer to it as my *studio*, and I even heard myself referring to it as the studio a few times before realizing I felt defensive about the lower status of gourd art. If *workshop* has been a good enough term for the space where I've made gourdcrafts and the Creative Force has made me, then it is good enough for the pottery space as well.

gourd girls

Ring Out the Grief

Our longtime close friend Mildred Neville, who had encouraged Janice and me so much over the years, had moved to Stevens Point, Wisconsin, in 1995 to study the viola, and eventually she started a stringed instrument business there. Although Mildred had returned to Georgia frequently since the move, we hadn't visited her new hometown. In the late summer of 2001, we'd at last made plans for the trip. The date of our flight just happened to be September 11.

As we drove into Atlanta on that terrible morning we heard the news of the World Trade Center attacks and airport closings. We turned around at the nearest exit and headed home. I'd never experienced such a mixture of shock, grief, and fear as when we heard those reports on the radio. And I'd never been so thankful to live in the protective shadow of Yonah.

Like everyone else, Janice and I understood in those first days that life as we had known it was over. In addition to fearing for our country, we feared for our own livelihood. We couldn't imagine that anyone would visit our place of business or buy anything from us in the future we now contemplated. Yet we did the only thing we knew to do, which was to go through the motions of life as we'd known it: we opened the shop and tried to work. Amazingly, some people came. Naturally there were tourists in northeast Georgia when the attacks took place, and they too went through the motions of vacationing and visiting attractions such as ours. People seemed thankful to escape the bad news even for a little while and to have their minds distracted; they even spent a little money. As the days wore on, we realized that people more than ever needed laughs, diversion, and creative inspiration. Perhaps we would still be able to make a living.

The first holiday season after the attacks was an emotional one and the beginning of new efforts on our part to reach out to visitors in a meaningful way. We realized as our Foothills Guild tour weekend approached that we wanted to find a theme to help us address the painful national and world situation. Some lines of poetry half-remembered from high school days began to haunt me until I identified their author and source. Written by Alfred Tennyson, the lines that became our theme for the season were part of his long poem *In Memoriam:*

> Ring out the grief that saps the mind,
> For those that here we see no more;
> Ring out the feud of rich and poor,
> Ring in redress to all mankind. . . .
>
> Ring out false pride in place and blood,
> The civic slander and the spite;
> Ring in the love of truth and right,
> Ring in the common love of good.

We hung a large gourd bell near our entrance, rung by a tiny gourd-head child who swung from the rope that moved the clapper. Tennyson's words were posted beside the scene, and copies were given to our visitors. We made special-edition bell ornaments for that year, from both gourds and clay. People appreciated our message and told us so. Since then a special theme has presented itself each year as we prepare for the holiday season, making the hectic period more meaningful for us and our visitors.

By December 2002 the U.S. invasion of Iraq was on the horizon. We chose world peace as our theme, and I wanted to make globe ornaments, each with a peace symbol engraved on the bottom. The task, which required that I carve all the continents and major islands on a planet the size of an orange, seemed absurdly difficult at first. But the experience of making the globes was magic for me, and they are special to those who now own them. Our handout was a song from the Unitarian Universalist hymnal called "Song of Peace."

Janice Lymburner

Ring out the grief

As 2003 neared its end, fear, stress, and a growing sense of division were taking their toll on Americans. It seemed as though the collective consciousness of our people was one of discouragement. We wanted to communicate a message of hope, of spring following winter; so I decided to carve special ornaments with gardens of brightly colored fantasy flowers. Each one was different, and on each was carved a brief quotation expressing the theme. Some words from Anne Morrow Lindburgh perhaps said it best: *Only with winter patience can we bring / The deep-desired, long-awaited spring.*

Our holiday theme in 2004, inspired by singer-songwriter Iris Dement's lyrics, was *Let the Mystery Be.* We wanted to point out the futility of humans arguing, attempting to oppress one another, or going to war for religious reasons. Special ornaments were gourds carved with Celtic knot designs, to me a reverent and appropriate symbol of mystery.

٭

Because of their great buoyancy, gourds have been used throughout history as floats for swimming and fishing. Several of our visitors have shared their memories of learning to swim with gourd "water wings."

I've never been a good swimmer myself, so it wasn't surprising that I wanted to bring gourd floats to our women's swimming group one evening in the summer of 2002. The group started when our close friend Rhev Tucker, who had begun doing water aerobics regularly for exercise, invited several friends to join her one evening a week in a community pool. Before going to the pool for the second gathering, Janice and I selected six or eight gourds as large as watermelons that we thought would hold us up in the water.

The women in the group were well acquainted with the gourd life, so they didn't even look surprised when Janice began pulling gourds out of large plastic garbage bags and asking them to humor me by trying them as floats. We all enjoyed clowning around with the gourds in the pool, pretending to perform Esther Williams–style synchronized swimming routines. Some waved the gourds in the air with mock grace while others of us clung to them to help stay afloat. Some tried to ride the slippery objects in the water horseback-style with varying degrees of success. We laughed hysterically when gourds popped out from under their riders and shot high into the air.

All of us were over 50, so we must have appeared an unlikely group to

Caroline Curran

In the pool with gourds from left Rhev Tucker, Linda Andersen, Carol Anne Lightsey, Susan Shlaer, Nannette Johnson, Kelly Williams, Priscilla and Janice, and Lynne Schwab

be acting so undignified—but we were having so much fun that we did-n't care what other swimmers thought of us. We proclaimed that folks who'd boasted of swimming with dolphins or manatees had nothing on us; *we* were swimming with *gourds!*

A few days after the first gourd swim a very witty member of the group called me and suggested that we needed an acronym. "Something about straights and lesbians swimming on gourds," she explained. The two of us brainstormed together and soon came up with SLUGS: Straight and Lesbian Unsynchronized Gourd Swimmers. The group loved the name, and it stuck.

We were good friends already, but with our new identity SLUGS became an even tighter group. When Janice and I adopted our puppies Cagney and Lacey in August, the group gave us a puppy shower complete with cake, balloons, and gifts such as old shoes. Soon SLUGS became a vehicle for organizing other strange and wonderful events.

In the fall we held a huge surprise birthday party at Nacoochee Presbyterian Church for our founder, Rhev Tucker, on the day she turned 75 ¾. Because her actual birthday is on December 26, no one had made much of a fuss for her 75th. We suggested that, because she was 75 and three-quarters, her friends might like to put quarters into a donation box that would go to a charity of Rhev's choice. Several hundred dollars were in the box after the party. We also presented Rhev with a "Queen of the Slugs" T-shirt and thus needed to explain our acronym to the community at large. Her three grown children in attendance wanted to make it known that Rhev is one of the *straight* members of the group.

After our fourth summer of swimming together, SLUGS are going strong. We share not only friendship and a belief in the wisdom of foolishness, but a special bond as an alliance of straight and lesbian women who cherish our diversity. For Janice and me the SLUGS group has been a delightful way of integrating the gourd life into the life of our beloved friends.

Gourdination

*I*n the early years of our business Janice and I realized with slight discomfort that people in the community called us *the gourd girls*. Folks began to slip and use the phrase in front of us, and then—sometimes sheepishly and sometimes with pride in their own perceived cleverness— admit it to us: "We call you the gourd girls. You don't mind, do you?" As the years went by, more and more individuals made this confession, each thinking she or he was the first to coin the phrase.

Once when the two of us were standing in front of a local church after a funeral, an elderly friend actually introduced us to an out-of-town mourner by saying in her soft, funeral-appropriate Southern drawl, "And these are our gourd girls." She said it as though every town had gourd girls —just as every town has firefighters or grocers. The poor woman being introduced to us, having no knowledge of this category of persons, was speechless.

I never especially liked being called *the gourd girls* for a couple of reasons. First, the label sounded bizarre to me—too much like *the goat man* or *the bird woman* or some such tag used throughout history to identify certain weird people with strange obsessions. We know our business is unusual but have never thought we belonged in the bizarre category.

Another problem I had with *gourd girls* was that people used it partly because they didn't know or care which one of us was Janice and which was Priscilla. "I can't tell you apart," they'd laugh, "and it doesn't matter anyway. To me you're just the gourd girls!" I began to understand the plight of twins who develop identity crises because no one knows which is which. "But I'm me!" I wanted to shout. "We are very different individuals! We don't even look anything alike!" I felt especially defensive on Janice's behalf and wanted to say, *"But can't you see she's the pretty one?"* No matter. We were *the gourd girls* and that was that.

This *gourd girl* designation was not something that seriously bothered us; it was just a conversation that we had to have repeatedly and in which we tried to be good sports. The exchanges became a little boring, like hearing the same joke again and again. Eventually we began finding some comic relief by describing our gourd girl label to people as an occupational hazard. Then the gourdination brought us to another level—but I'm getting ahead of myself.

During the 2002 SLUG summer we had to say goodbye to Patty Workman, who had been helping us off and on for more than 10 years, when she learned she was expecting her second child. A talented artist in her own right, Patty had been a stabilizing force for Janice and me through our hardest times, always pleasant, dependable, competent, and creative. We weren't sure how we would manage without her.

As we tried to imagine who might fill Patty's shoes, we thought of Liesel Potthast, an acquaintance whom we liked and knew to be a hard worker. Liesel had emigrated to the United States from Germany in 1985 with her husband and small son, Patrick. She had been through a divorce a few years later and had worked hard to support herself and Patrick for 15 years. She'd been self-employed as a house cleaner during that time and had earned an excellent reputation. But at the time we approached her about a part-time job her life was changing. Happily remarried and re-examining her life, Liesel was ready to pursue a new challenge of some kind.

An artistic person herself, she had dabbled in various craft forms and was especially drawn to our gourd pottery. She liked the idea of helping Janice in the retail shop as well. She decided to give the job a try.

Within days Janice and I saw Liesel for the magical pixie that she is. *Pixie* was definitely the word that came to mind, even though Liesel is of average size. She was cute, fun, and a quick study, both in the workshop and with customers. Within weeks we could see that she was having a profoundly positive influence on us. Although the influx of energy and good feelings generated by Gourd Impressions had pulled us out of our malaise of the late 1990s, there were still times when our energies and enthusiasm lagged. So when Liesel became irrepressibly excited about our brainchild, we saw it again through different eyes and found fresh appreciation for the phenomenon we had created.

As the end of Liesel's first year with us approached, Janice and I decided to have a party for her around the anniversary date and hold a gourdination ceremony: a combination graduation and ordination in which she would be officially installed as a gourd girl. Although both Carey and Patty had also in effect been gourd girls, we never had the idea for a gourdination until 2003.

At first our purposes were to honor Liesel and to give ourselves an excuse to stage an extravaganza in the tradition of past gourd gatherings. But when we focused on the task of creating an actual gourdination ceremony, we realized that, as silly and laughable as this rite of passage might be, the act of conferring the title "gourd girl" upon another person was very meaningful to us as a way of embracing and celebrating our own gourd girl identities.

We told Liesel simply that we were having an outdoor potluck party to celebrate her one-year anniversary with us, but she sensed that we had something up our sleeves. After the crowd of 100 had eaten and socialized, Janice and I appeared on the deck above the crowd in our so-called gourd girl ceremonial garb: necklaces and earrings made from large, teardrop-shaped gourds; tall wizard-like gourd hats; and Groucho Marx masks. During the singing of the opening song, "When You Wish upon a Gourd," we escorted the candidate from the audience to our makeshift stage.

We then narrated and acted out the story of Liesel's "epic quest for gourd girl status," which included her assignments to "untie the gourdian knot" and remove the "gourd-in-the-stone." Her third and most difficult task, according to our tale, was winning the hearts of her fairy gourdmothers, who "turned out to be just queer, neurotic gourd girls in disguise." The narration concluded:

> Somehow, despite all the difficult challenges, Liesel managed
> to win the hearts of the gourd girls. They were inspired and
> uplifted by her enthusiasm for the gourd life. They were

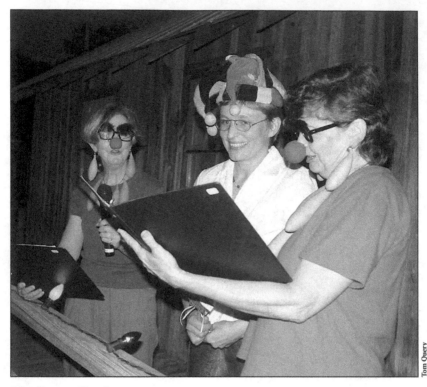

Tom Query

Liesel's gourdination

enchanted by her sweet and generous nature. They were wowed by her quick mind and amazing work ethic. In short, they wanted to gourdain her as a fellow gourd girl.

At this point Liesel was asked to take her vows:

—Do you promise to accept as gracefully as possible the indignity of being called a gourd girl?
—Do you promise to keep *trying* to appreciate gourd puns in English?
—And, finally, do you, understanding that the gourd life is really about following your heart, promise to continue being a gourd girl as long as you want to but no longer?

Liesel gave the desired answers—quite seriously, much to our satisfaction. Janice placed a special "crown" on her head—a jester's hat with flashing lights and gourd baubles, and the audience joined in singing Beethoven and Schiller's "Ode to Joy" in German. Liesel in turn gave Janice and me flowers and moving thank-you speeches.

For that evening the hard times were forgotten: the failed crops, the years in the closet, the struggles to build a business and to support ourselves. It was a magical night, a night when "gourd girl" seemed like the most wonderful and honorable title a person might grow up to claim.

gourd girls

The Gourd 'Uns

We three gourd girls continued our journey into the gourd life. Liesel became involved in almost every aspect of the business and was always as excited as we were about any new project we tackled. I made her a T-shirt printed with the words *Ich bin ein gourd girl,* which gave everyone smiles.

Soon after the Gourdination the three of us had declared Liesel's husband Dan Calhoun president and sole member of the Gourd Girls' Auxiliary (GGA). A cute redhead whose wit and appearance make his Irish heritage apparent, Dan understood the significance of the gourd life and was an enthusiastic supporter even before the Gourdination. He took his responsibility as the lone GGA member seriously and helped us in many ways, especially by regularly hauling pottery-making supplies from Atlanta, where he commutes to work. At the end of 2004 we began a tradition of holding an annual Gourd Girls' Auxiliary Awards Dinner to honor him.

In 2005 Dan distinguished himself even further by saving the pond on our property after the corroding standpipe broke and was allowing the water to drain away. Janice and I located a two-foot-in-diameter galvanized culvert pipe to place over the broken one, but we didn't have the strength or the know-how to apply this heavy and unwieldy bandaid.

Anne Ripley Vann

The Gourd 'Uns

We turned to Dan, who happens to be a hydrologist by profession, for help. Even with Liesel, Janice, and me all trying to assist, the job proved to be extremely difficult; after he had worked for almost an hour to get the pipe seated in the bottom of the lake, I began worrying that Dan would hurt himself and pleaded with him to give up. Not only did he persevere until he succeeded in securing the new pipe, but he did it in spite of my near-hysterical attempts to stop him.

We ecstatically dubbed him a hero and tried to name the lake after him, but there Dan drew the line. Even as president of the GGA he didn't want this dubious accolade. As he put it, "Imagine what Sidney Lanier would have thought about his name being applied to a clog in the stream that flowed so beautifully out of the Hills of Habersham."

In January of 2005 we began making something that I never expected: gourdhead dolls. The catalyst had been a friend who commissioned me the previous summer to make a doll for her to give as a special gift. It was rather primitive-looking but had a curious charm, especially after our friend dressed it in real children's clothes bought at a yard sale. Everyone who saw it fell in love, and the SLUGS in particular encouraged us to make dolls to sell.

Throughout the busy fall season, when I had no time for developing a new product, I fantasized about creating a line of characters that would bring into three-dimensional form some of the gourd puns we'd been collecting for years. I loved the idea of making Little Gourdy Two-Shoes, Gourdgie Porgie, Flash Gourdon, and others as toddler-sized soft sculpture dolls. Janice and I had seen a few gourdhead dolls made by other artists over the years, but none were anything like the Gourd 'Uns, as we came to call them.

Periodically I talked excitedly to Janice and Liesel about the dolls. Liesel's usual enthusiasm was lacking, and Janice was downright negative about the idea. She was concerned that, because our county was already famous for Cabbage Patch Kids, people would think we were trying to piggyback on their success. I reminded her that dolls had existed for thousands of years before the Kids came along and that ours would be completely different in concept and appearance from the Cabbage Patch characters. Although I still agree that we have an unfortunate coincidence to overcome in marketing the Gourd 'Uns, I wasn't willing to let that stop me from doing something that felt so life-giving.

After we closed the store for the winter I bought yards of tea-dyed muslin and bags of fiber-fill. Ceasing my campaign to sell Janice on the doll idea, I began sewing bodies, stuffing them, and figuring out how to attach the heads and make the hair. All the while I watched her out of the corner of my eye. Unlike me, Janice had dearly loved playing with dolls as a child, and I knew she'd be unable to resist these.

I was right: before long, she was going into town regularly to shop for used baby clothes at thrift stores, trying different outfits and accessories on the Gourd 'Uns, and instructing me on which clothes worked best for which character. Flash Gourdon, for example, wore a running suit and shoes that lit up. Gourdilocks wore a dress with three bears on it, and Gourd of the Jungle sported elephants and a safari hat. For Mr. Gourdwrench Janice found a pair of coveralls with tools embroidered on the front. Eventually we had 20 different characters.

Liesel, too, became enthusiastic when she saw how Janice was bringing the dolls to life. She and I were both thrilled that Janice, who'd always given me too much credit for being the creative partner, had found her own medium. Sales of the Gourd 'Uns didn't set the world on fire right away, but for me their creation was wonderfully satisfying. Unable as usual to resist a chance to proselytize about the gourd life, I wrote a brief characterization for the cards that accompany each doll:

> The Gourd 'Uns are soft, cuddly, and endearingly empty-headed; thus they are free of mental clutter, vanity, and self-importance. But they can be quite thick-skulled when it comes to protecting the environment. They come from the earth, and they know it—so they insist on wearing recycled clothes and natural fiber hair. They'd like to remind all their new friends to choose the simple life and love our planet.

gourd girls

American Dreams

I was the "baby" in my family. My parents and older brother and sister all preached to me from the time I was small about the importance of being an individual. I can still hear them at the supper table in chorus: "Don't just follow the crowd." "Be yourself." "Be different." My mother loved to quote from Polonius' speech to his son Laertes in Hamlet: "This above all, to thine own self be true," she'd intone solemnly, tapping her fingernail on the table, "and it must follow as the night the day thou canst not then be false to any man."

My family made me feel good about being left-handed and double-jointed—even about my lack of common sense, because that always made them laugh. They helped open my heart to whoever I might become if I could be true to myself—but maybe I went a little overboard. Who knew I would turn out to be a *lesbian* in the *gourd* business, of all things?

Some days now when I look back on 29 years of living the gourd life with Janice, I am amazed at our good fortune. Other days we both wonder if somewhere along the line our dream became a sort of dream-nightmare hologram. Now you see it, now you don't; this moment it's a dream, the next, a nightmare.

Why is it that some of us can't let go when dreams begin to cross that shifting line into nightmare territory? How does one know when or if it's time to let go? I've never been able to make that call, but my own experience of hanging on is that sooner or later something always happens to give our dream new life, and that maybe it makes better sense to stay with the same dream than to start over with a new one. I've come to believe, at least in good times, that Janice and I have made a kind of spiritual practice of staying the course. Janice mostly agrees but says I think way too much.

I do wonder more and more frequently with age, like most people: What is the meaning of our story? Why might it be worthwhile to write down or to read? My belief is that the redeeming value in telling such a personal tale is in acknowledging the unseen struggles that all of us live, even those of us engaged in whimsy. Everyone spends time in one kind of closet or another, and we give each other comfort when we're willing to share our lives in an honest way.

🦌

Not long ago, Janice and I went for a hike to see the Vasey's trillium blooming on one of our favorite wildflower trails an hour's drive north of us in Rabun County. Afterward, as I drove us east on Betty's Creek Road back toward Highway 441, we were listening for the first time to a CD by singer-songwriter Iris Dement. A beautiful song called "After You're Gone" blind-sided us, the words sounding as though either of us could have written them to the other. We both fell silent as we listened:

> There'll be laughter even after you're gone.
> I'll find reasons and I'll face that empty dawn.
> 'Cause I've memorized each line in your face,
> And not even death could ever erase the stories
>   they tell to me.

We held hands tightly, tears standing in our eyes. I wondered for the millionth time which of us would die first and leave the other behind. Yet even in that moment of imagined grief, I was filled with gratitude for the stories.

Afterword

Many of the people who came back to life briefly in these pages, including some of our special GAGG friends, have been dead for years. I have loved being with them again as I've relived our story.

Our corner of northeast Georgia has changed dramatically since we planted the first crop of gourds in 1977. Like every attractive part of the southern United States, our area is being flooded with people who can't be blamed for simply wanting to live in a pretty place. Janice and I count ourselves lucky that we were able to know the county and some of its exceptionally fine people before time and bulldozers began taking their toll.

Some of the wildflowers we planted 14 years ago—and felt so discouraged about—have finally begun to take hold. The fire pinks have established themselves in one area near the lake, columbines beside wild geraniums in another spot, and dwarf crested iris in another. Along a creek bank in the woods, the number of trout lilies slowly increases year by year. They refuse to be rushed, but their continuation is assured now; I imagine them blooming in profusion long after we're not around to see them.

And so the wildflower-pottery-gourd life continues. It holds new adventures, new ways to be foolish—and, yes, financial worries as well. I'd like to say I've learned to have faith, but the truth is that I'm painfully slow to learn that lesson. I do know the odds are in our favor: a business that has stayed afloat (there's that metaphor again) for 29 years will most likely remain so.

The truth is—and I'm not just whistling in the dark here—that the kind of economic pressure we've encountered, even with its accompanying fear and pain, has been a kind of blessing. Had Janice and I inherited a fortune fifteen years ago, our creative lives would likely have ended then; so in a sense we have been much richer with financial challenge as a catalyst than we would have been without.

It seems to me that we Americans have a curious way of ascribing almost magical qualities to artists and their work; hence my own inabilty to claim that label *artist* for many years. My experiences have taught me to see artistic ability and creativity as two "muscle groups" that can work in conjunction with one another or separately. Like actual muscles, they are strengthened by exercise and purposeful use. Every human being has these muscles and the ability to develop them in surprising ways.

———

As for Nacoochee Presbyterian Church, it continues to be a strong and inspiring witness for equality within the Presbyterian Church (U.S.A.). Janice remains active, often participating in worship services as a liturgist or by leading the Time with Children. Adults as well as children love to hear her bring the scriptures to life with stories and participatory activities.

Bob Prim, the minister who was called after John Hobbs' departure, has proven himself to be a courageous and untiring advocate for equality, as have parish associates Joy White Pruett, Keith Nickle, and Gerald Jenkins. All of them as well as many new members who've joined the church in recent years—gay, lesbian, and straight—have come to Nacoochee in part because they want to belong to a Christian community that is inclusive. Janice's early influence has made a difference to everyone associated with this amazing little church in the valley.

Unfortunately the picture is more complicated for gays and lesbians in the United States at large. Because of the information and support available to them, many young people today are coming out of the closet in their teens or 20s. Yet they are doing so at a time when there is an outpouring of judgment against gay and lesbian people. We are seen as fair game in a seemingly endless public debate about our nature, our morality, our worthiness of the right to form legal partnerships and carry on normal, respectable lives.

Janice and I feel a deep sadness and weariness when we think of all the good people who see us as a threat, an evil suddenly being thrust on society. What I have been saying, even in these words of our offbeat gourd girl story, is that gays and lesbians have been right here beside you all along—growing gourds, providing medical care, repairing appliances, teaching school, fighting fires, being your friends and neighbors—all of it. We want—and deserve—the same things from life that everyone else wants: the chance to know the joy and comfort of sharing our lives with loving partners, opportunities to contribute, the privilege of a spiritual search, lessons in the wisdom of foolishness.

I dedicate this book to Janice Lymburner, the love of my life.

Acknowledgments

I am deeply grateful to the many people who so generously helped bring this book into being. In order of their involvement with the book:

Janice Lymburner held me in her heart yet unfailingly gave me tough, honest feedback throughout the sometimes difficult experience of revisiting the past.

My brother, Bill Wilson, who read and critiqued some of my earliest efforts, expected me to be a better writer than I am and thus made me try harder to write well.

Mildred Neville encouraged me beyond belief with her friendship, unshakeable conviction that the book was worth writing, beautiful enthusiasm, and insightful editing help.

Lilith Quinlan spent many hours helping me to envision the book and to find my narrative voice as well as giving me valuable feedback.

Elsa Ann Gaines gave me confidence as a writer and helped me believe that our story could be a car, not just a bicycle.

John Kollock advised me on all kinds of issues and kept his heart open despite our philosophical differences.

Liesel Potthast understood my vision for the book and patiently and compassionately endured my constant chatter as we worked together in the workshop.

Matt Gedney cheerfully answered dozens of questions about self-publishing and even gave me one of his ISBN numbers.

My stepmother, Berenice Wilson, became the first reader of a complete draft and gave me tremendous encouragement, insightful feedback, and practical help.

My father, Bill Wilson, freely and lovingly gave the first draft his approval and blessing, without which I would not have been comfortable telling our story so openly.

Janice's mother and stepfather, Nancy and Don Webb, gave me constant support, encouragement, and sympathy.

Karen Dunn and Lynne Hagstrom of Stevens Point, Wisconsin, served as "cold" readers (no pun intended!) and gave me hope that our story might interest someone beyond northeast Georgia.

Barbara Williams shared her great editing talents and fine instincts with me, becoming my generous advocate, frank critic, and mainstay during the final six months.

Sam Williams made our book real to us by drafting a preliminary cover and naming the book in the process.

Patsey Parker became my friend and spent many hours reading the first draft and sharing her insights.

Carol Majors patiently and unselfishly answered hundreds of questions about self-publishing, shared valuable resources, and helped us to make good decisions.

Emory Jones generously gave of his time and talent as a photographer just because he "likes to help his neighbors," though we barely knew each other at the start.

Linda Crittenden made me her friend for life as she freely shared her talent as a graphic designer, her perfectionism, and her inspiring love of learning, spending untold hours bringing the book to life and making it reader-friendly.

Catherine Cottingham donated her amazing professional copy-editing talents during the final stages of production and made Gourd Girls a much better book.

Finally, the SLUGS and many more special friends cared about the book, asked about its progress, listened, and listened some more.

Janice and I also want to thank the many people whose special roles in the gourd life I was unable to describe individually in these pages, including all the beloved members of GAGG; all the people who have cleaned gourds for us or helped us in the shop; and all the people who have been so generous for 29 years with their words of encouragement and their purchases.